dixi
books

Pete Barker

Pete grew up in the English countryside with a deep appreciation of nature and realising the harm humans are doing to it, he joined Greenpeace to be a volunteer activist, taking part in campaigns and direct actions for the environment. He has now drawn on these remarkable experiences and those of close colleagues to form an exciting compilation of true stories.

Writing credits include blogs for Greenpeace and Plane Stupid, winner of a Flash 500 competition, published in Aftermath Magazine and a debut novel.

Pete now lives off grid in a straw bale house he designed and built with his wife, and 20 Angora rabbits in rural Wales.

PS. the rabbits were hopeless at house building.

Author website: www.viewfromabridge.yolasite.com

20 RIOT COPS TO NICK 2 CHICKENS

by Pete Barker
with Anthony Perrett (Arctic 30), Janet Barker and Friends

dixi
books

Dixi Books

Copyright © 2022 by Pete Barker
Copyright © 2022 Dixi Books
All rights reserved. No part of this book may be used or reproduced or transmitted to any form or by any means, electronic or mechanical, including photocopying, recording, or by any information and retrieval system, without written permission from the Publisher.

20 Riot Cops to Nick 2 Chickens
Pete Barker
Editor: Andrea Bailey
Designer: Pablo Ulyanov
Cover Design: Nick Oliver
I. Edition: November 2022

Library of Congress Cataloging-in-Publication Data
Pete Barker - 1st ed.
ISBN: 978-1-913680-56-5
1. Ecology 2. Activisim 3. Environmental Action

Printed by Short Run Press, Exeter, Devon.
© Dixi Books Publishing
293 Green Lanes, Palmers Green, London, N13 4XS, England
info@dixibooks.com
www.dixibooks.com

FSC
www.fsc.org
MIX
Paper from responsible sources
FSC® C014540

20 RIOT COPS TO NICK 2 CHICKENS

by Pete Barker
with Anthony Perrett (Arctic 30), Janet Barker and Friends

dixi books

The Voice of the New Age

This book is dedicated to protectors of nature the world over, in particular those who have lost their lives following their moral compass.

Contents

Preface by John Sauven 11

Introduction 15

The Rainbow Warrior 17

The Red Carpet 26

Shutting Down Kingsnorth Power Station 33

No Dash for Gas 46

Plane Stupid 54

An Activist's Story 59

BP or not BP? 73

Liberate Tate 77

Anthony of the Arctic 80

Zaharah's Story 117

NVDA – Nonviolent Direct Action 122

Breaking the Law 125

The Kidlington Airport Debacle 126

Shell Garages 132

A Climbing Action 140

The Gift of Solar 146

Brussels 148

PNR Bake Off	153
Boxupants	163
The Woman in the Red Dress	180
Extinction Rebellion	188
Insulate Britain	191
A Trojan Horse	194
The Oil Rig	200
Afterword	211
Acknowledgements	213

Preface

As I write this I will have been with Greenpeace for over three decades – yes a life sentence! But looking back over 30 years of activism there is both optimism and desperation. The desperation revealed in the young climate activists on whose heads our failures will fall. The optimism because 30 years of activism has achieved results even if they are not yet at the scale we need.

As one pundit said we are entering a deeply confusing decade when our response to the climate crisis will get better (hopefully in deeds and not just words) and the climate and nature crisis itself will get a lot worse.

So where is the optimism? This book shows the courage, creativity and strength of an extraordinary range of individuals who have stood up to the most powerful polluters on this planet. The awareness that has been raised and the pressure that has been applied is having an impact.

It's not yet at the speed and scale of say the Covid response. The G7 countries alone spent over $12tn on support for its citizens and businesses during Covid. Imagine if just a portion of that was spent on the climate emergency. But Covid did at least show it could be done! Where there is a will, there is a way.

Civilisation has thrived in what has been termed a bountiful garden of Eden for 10,000 years and we are about to leave it for a new destination not seen for millions of years. Hence everyone is now waking up a bit late after the party with a hangover and reaching for the net zero pill. Of course, three decades ago all the world leaders went to Rio for an Earth Summit and pledged to act on the climate crisis, end biodiversity loss and pursue sustainable development

(Agenda 21). The sad fact is that since the Rio Earth Summit in 1992 the world has emitted more carbon dioxide than it has in the entire preceding sweep of human civilisation. Action not words, as Greenpeace said at the time on a banner at the top of Nelson's column in Trafalgar Square, is still what counts.

We now have one decade to cut emissions in half and get to net zero before mid-century. As Professor Rockstrom said that's ten times round the sun and we must be well on the way to solving the climate and nature emergency. Basically, that means getting off fossil fuels and switching to a predominantly plant-based diet.

But every fraction of a degree of warming that is averted will save lives and improve humanity's prospects, even as climate impacts worsen. And it's not all doom and gloom. The good news is that the transition to net zero is feasible and far cheaper than most feared even a decade ago. If one considers all the other potential benefits including cleaner air, greener jobs, healthier lifestyles, less inequality etc then making the transition is a 'no-brainer.'

Since the Rio Earth Summit in '92, environmental activists have both raised the alarm and delivered real change on the ground. Perhaps not remembered or sufficiently recognised but Greenpeace were in at the start of the UK offshore wind industry with the development at North Hoyle in 2003. Today the UK is the world's No 1 offshore wind power.

Four years later, in 2007, we took the battle to Kingsnorth in Kent to stop a new coal fired power station being built. Maybe hard to believe now but polluting coal plants like Kingsnorth supplied a third of the UK's electricity, and the government was considering plans to build new ones across the country. Renewables were supplying less than 6% of our electricity. Most people had never seen an electric vehicle let alone an offshore wind farm. Much of the rest of the world was on a coal-building boom. But Greenpeace, later joined by a huge coalition of environmental and development organisations, forced the government to accept a coal phase-out by 2025 (later brought forward to 2024).

Greenpeace also started a new frontier oil campaign in the Arctic in 2010 with an action against a little-known Scottish oil driller Cairn Energy in Greenland. Later we took on Shell in the Arctic and ultimately the Russian government. Shell pulled out. The Russian government is another story. Even with an old foe like BP the dam finally broke. In 2019 the oil giant served several high court injunctions to stop Greenpeace taking action against the company's attempt to drill new oil wells in the North Sea. The injunctions I ignored, dodging jail but landing a big fine our supporters generously paid for. Then in August 2020 – more than a month earlier than expected – BP announced plans to slash oil and gas production by 2030 and deliver 50 gigawatts of renewable electricity.

Even the International Energy Agency called for an end to new fossil fuel projects if the world wanted a 50% chance of meeting the 1.5-degree C target (and they were set up to promote fossil fuels!).

When it comes to the other side of the same coin – nature on land and at sea – the story over the last three decades is not too dissimilar. Humans and livestock now account for nearly 96 per cent of the mammals on the planet. The world's food system accounts for around a third of all greenhouse gas emissions with industrial agriculture and especially intensive animal agriculture being particularly destructive. Livestock production requires large amounts of forested land to be cleared to create space for grazing cattle or to grow animal feed like soya. The only solution is a wholesale switch to a more plant-based diet, containing more fruit and vegetables and less meat and dairy. In addition to stopping the destruction of ecosystems, humans must go further by rewilding and restoring degraded land and ocean environments. And, perhaps more than anything, supporting indigenous groups to protect the earth.

As Greta said: "We can no longer let people in power decide what hope is. Hope is not passive. Hope is not 'blah blah blah.' Hope is telling the truth. Hope is taking action. And hope always comes from the people."

John Sauven
CEO
Greenpeace UK
February 22nd 2022

Introduction

There comes a time in life when all the fine words and good intentions just don't cut it anymore and you have to get off your arse and get things done.

This is why I became an environmental activist towards the end of the first decade of the twenty-first century. Joining the Poole and Bournemouth Greenpeace group, I threw myself into learning and campaigning for the ecosystems that maintain life on Earth. The more I found out, the more I realised the scale of the problem and the more committed I became.

The tipping point for me came one afternoon when I was at work, taking a tea break. Janet, my girlfriend at the time; who later became my wife, had hinted she was on a mission so I checked the internet news and was hit by the headline, "*20 Riot Cops to Nick 2 Chickens.*" My mouth dried as I scanned down the article. It was about a Greenpeace action at the McDonalds in central Manchester, along with others across the country, highlighting that chicken sold by the chain was being fed on soya from cleared Amazonian rainforest. Around the corner had been a high profile conference, hence the riot police. Two activists dressed as seven foot chickens had 'locked on' – chaining themselves to tables inside the restaurant.

If I had to identify a single point in time that I fell in love with Janet, it was the moment I saw her name, she was one of the chickens arrested. Her principles hit my heart hard. Now it was my turn to step up.

That's it in a nutshell. I could go on for ages, going into the love of nature, the atrocities people do and the miracles too, but I won't. Other people can write that stuff better than me, so I will just share with you a few of the remarkable experiences that I and people close to me, have been involved in.

This book is a collection of events adapted into stories using a variety of styles and voices. These are true stories, told from firsthand accounts and my own experiences, although most of the details are accurate, some have had to be changed for reasons of security, narrative or memory. Some of the dialogue is accurate, some has been created to carry the story along. I have usually kept to first names only to protect identities and sometimes changed them entirely if there may be legal ramifications. Please forgive these vagaries and aberrations, they are done to provide the reader with a complete and enjoyable experience.

I've written this book to show how ordinary people find the resolve to do some pretty odd things and why. Perhaps it will also encourage others to write their stories, I know there are so many tales of drama, bravery and humour waiting to be retold. But most of all, I hope this book inspires people to get off their arses, step out of their comfort zone and do what needs to be done.

The Rainbow Warrior

"The *Rainbow Warrior* is coming to the UK for three weeks and we have two volunteer places available on board."

That is the email message from Greenpeace and my innards are bouncing up and down. The *Rainbow Warrior II*, perhaps the most famous ship of all time, is coming and I can apply. I know the chances are slim, supporters up and down the country will be jumping at the opportunity but I may as well give it a go. I check I have enough annual leave and phone my girlfriend.

Janet has been active in the organisation since she was thirteen, fundraising at first and when she left university, a stint interning at the London office. It was she who encouraged me to join the local group.

'You know, you'll probably not get on,' she says.

'I know, but do you think it's worth trying?'

'Of course it is. I was offered a place on the *Arctic Sunrise* once but had to turn it down because I was starting a new job.'

'Why don't you apply too?'

'Can't get time off work. No, you go for it.'

'Okay, no harm in trying. I do have some experience sailing tall ships, Competent Crew and Day Skipper certificates as well, might help.'

'If you get it, I'll not talk to you for a month.'

'I'll have my phone, I can call—'

'No, I mean I won't want to talk to you.'

I'm at work, keeping an eye on a temperamental machine on an automatic production line when I feel my phone vibrating in my pocket. London number.

'Hi, it's Rachael at Greenpeace. Pete, you've got the deckhand place on the *Warrior*.'

'You're joking.'

'I'm not. You're keen, you've got sailing experience. How do you feel about writing for the website, an onboard blog sort of thing?'

'Yeah, I think I can do that.'

'Great, I'll send you a letter with all the details.'

I'm tingling, can't stop smiling, silently screaming inside. I need to book the time off and phone Janet.

'Janet, I got the place. I'm only going on the *Rainbow Warrior*!'

Silence.

'Janet?'

'Bastard.'

'You, you don't mind do you?'

'It's what I've always wanted and you get it.'

'Sorry.'

'Don't be. But if you go off with some pretty deckhand, I will hunt you down.'

I'm walking down East India Dock and there she is. Bigger than I imagined. The deep green of the hull and the familiar dove of peace logo with the name Greenpeace in white trailing down the side. My heart is in my mouth as I take a photo of the bow. There's a lot of activity on deck so I call out to introduce myself. Penny, the Bosun, greets me:

'What brings you to the *Warrior*?' She is mid-forties with long, blonde hair that could have been sun-bleached light brown, tall, and a face you instantly warm to. Penny is in charge of the deck and will be my "line manager" in lubber terms.

'I'm a volunteer, from the Bournemouth Greenpeace group.'

'Ah, you're family then.'

She hands me over to Alex and we're asked to clean up some rusty tools. As we step inside the fo'c'sle, I notice the bulkhead covered in campaign stickers going right back to the anti-nuclear testing days. I'm glad to be out of the hubbub and have something to keep me busy. The crew is multi-national but Alex is English and well spoken, he tells me about his father who will be coming to visit soon. We get along from the start with similar quiet personalities.

Later I'm given a bunk, sharing a cabin below deck with Alex and Amrit and introduced to Anthony who is the other UK volunteer. He will be the assistant cook for the next three weeks and is busy carving a boot print, the same as the campaign logo, in the side of a pumpkin in time for Halloween.

I slip into shipboard routine. Harbour watches, daily cleaning and assisting at evening receptions for VIPs and high value donors. Every couple of days, I write a short piece for the Greenpeace website, giving a personal perspective to the ship's visit and building momentum for the open boat days. This is when the public are allowed onboard and given tours. Crew who are confident in English are allocated positions to present short talks about whatever's around them. For some unfathomable reason, I'm put on the bridge. This is the ship's control room. Windows all round give 360 degree vision. Behind me, as I perch on the Captain's chair, is a deck of instruments including the joystick steering and engine throttle. On either side of the bridge are doors, port and starboard, and in the centre, stairs leading below.

Before the first tour I'm desperately grabbing any crew member I can find to tell me something I can talk about. The controls, the radar, charts and even flags. "The binoculars are for looking through." Really! Who'd have known?

I'm stiff with nerves as the first group of twenty people are funnelled towards me. They settle in around the various bits of equipment, looking at me expectantly. At that moment I catch Mike's eye as he pops his head into the Bridge.

'Ah, let me introduce the Captain,' I say, praying I won't be told off for being presumptuous. Thankfully Mike enjoys telling a good story and launches into the one about the time French commandos boarded the ship as it sailed into an exclusion zone to stop a nuclear test. Breaking into the bridge, they tried to stop the ship but nothing happened. They ripped out the electronics but the ship sailed on into the test area. It took them thirty hours before discovering the captain, up a mast, sitting in the crows nest, steering the ship by remote control.

From that point on, to every group that comes around, I explain the controls, the charts, radar and retell Mike's story.

After a couple of weeks, we move from London to Southend-on-Sea. This is the *Give Coal the Boot* tour and just down the coast is Kingsnorth Power Station, an ageing coal-fired plant. There are plans to build a new one next door, the first of many in the UK, unless we can kick up such a stink that the government will see the grave error they were allowing. Coal is cheap and plentiful but also the greatest contributor of greenhouse gasses in the atmosphere. To carry on burning more, at this scale, would be a death sentence to countless lives.

We moor up at the end of the mile long pier. A small train brings visitors for the open boat day and that evening, Alex, Amrit and myself borrow push bikes to cycle into town to watch a Cohen Brothers movie at the cinema.

The next day and we know mischief is afoot. People are arriving, campaigners, photographers and Patrick. It's no surprise to learn that we are taking the *Warrior* to the power station. All afternoon, activists are arriving in twos and threes, trying to look innocent as they board the mini train with rucksacks. We cannot be sure that we're being watched but expect the police are keeping an eye on us. Roughly thirty volunteers are now onboard along with a Dutch canoe team. My Janet is with them, having trained in the Netherlands. It's the first time I've seen her in two weeks and I rush up to give her a big hug. It will be so nice to have her around tonight but there is a lot to do and she insists on hanging out with her Dutch team mates.

Evening briefing. We are going to Kingsnorth Power Station. The new one, we are told, will be producing the same amount of CO_2 as thirty of the lowest emitting countries combined. Some of these countries are also the first to be impacted by climate change. The primary objective is to block the arrival of a shipment of coal by docking the *Warrior* at the power station jetty. Patrick explains the second objective to the newly arrived volunteers in a packed mess (dining/lounge area):

'You all have to stay hidden in here, because when we tie up to the jetty, IF we tie up to the jetty, they must not suspect we've got something else planned.' Behind him is a sheet with a rough drawing of the power station. 'Each of you will be given a flag of one of the thirty nations and when the tide comes in, at roughly midday, you will all come pouring out and leap onto the quay, but you've got to be quick so they can't stop you.'

'Leap onto the quay?' someone asks.

Silence in the room while Patrick looks down, trying not to smile. 'We might put a plank out for you,' he says.

Turning to the drawing, he points to a dotted line. 'John will then lead you through the power station and out the other side to the field where the new one is due to be built. There will be a short ceremony to bear witness, John will read a statement and you plant the flags.'

'Do you think they'll let us just walk through?'

'No. We'll actually get better photos if they stop you somewhere along here,' Patrick says pointing halfway along the route. 'Although the stated intention is to walk through.'

At the back of the room, one woman is looking a bit pale, she's still thinking about walking the plank.

That night Alex comes up to me and says, 'This time, it feels like it's for real.'

I nod but inside, I don't understand. He has been involved in actions on the *Warrior* for at least three months. Is it because it's now on home territory or because we are actually going to stop a delivery of dirty coal? I should have asked because as I lie in my bunk, trying to sleep, his words keep bumping up, riding tiny waves of adrenaline.

I'm out of my bunk at 3.45am for an early watch. A couple of hours later, the ship's four RHIBs (rigid hulled, inflatable boats) are being launched and coming up the coast are three London based boats. We cast off and are all moving. The radar picking out a line of eight vessels all going at full speed in the same direction, to Kingsnorth.

Mike, the Captain, is informed by the Coast Guard that he will be breaking maritime law if he does not stop to take on a pilot. He replies that he cannot as it would put a fellow mariner's career at risk and keeps going.

John Sauven, the Greenpeace UK Executive Director, is on the bridge, telephone in hand. He is calling the head of E.ON in the UK, telling him we are going to his power station. Binoculars are searching the shoreline for police boats but none appear. We're on deck, craning for our first sighting of the chimney.

Through the morning mist rising over the fens, we see it. Not far now, just around the headland.

As we approach the jetty we can see a large police patrol boat holding position at the far end. Mike throttles right back and we drift past the police. On the blind side of the *Warrior*, the Dutch team, including Janet, slip the inflatable canoes into the water and start paddling for the jetty. Their job is to land people on the rust encrusted rungs running up the dockside and help secure mooring lines.

Mike brings the ship to a stop, allowing the incoming tide to gently push her backwards. He steers to starboard, turning stern first then bringing the bow around in a 180 degree arc. Thereby placing the ship in front of the patrol boat and drifting into the jetty.

I'm at the stern with two other crew, ready to pass out the thick mooring lines.

The police start powering forwards to block our way, pushing the canoes aside. It looks like they are going to be able to just shuffle up and down stopping our every move. Then around the end of the quay a little miracle appears. A dingy with the message, "NO NEW COAL" written on its sail. It swings around in front of the patrol boat, international law of the sea, power gives way to sail. The police stop and two of our RHIBs are given the signal to push the *Warrior* up to the jetty.

As the dingy clears away, I see the bow mooring line thrown to canoeists who attach it to a pillar supporting the jetty. We manage to get a line to one of our small inflatable boats but it cannot manoeuvre easily in the rapidly diminishing space, so they quickly tie it off and escape as the police boat once again edges forward. We watch, powerless, as an officer leans over the front rail of the launch and with a very sharp knife, cuts through the thick rope. Mike is not happy, cutting a mooring line is a really irresponsible thing to do. The rope is hauled in, canoes appear and it's quickly passed out, further up the ship, to a couple who bravely paddle between the ship and the jetty to loop around a pillar that the police cannot reach. We're on, and hauling ourselves in towards the jetty as the canoes slip away.

Beyond the end of the quay, is a small, square, stone and wooden island known as a dolphin. Patrick, Anthony, Lucas and a couple of climbers jump into an RHIB with a massive projector, taking it to the dolphin so later, when darkness falls, they can project a video onto the side of the power station.

Lucas is passing supplies up for an extended occupation of the dolphin when a police RHIB approaches.

'STOP THAT,' they shout. Lucas carries on.

There are other boats whizzing around so the police go to find someone who might take notice of them.

The next delivery to the dolphin is a brand new 7kva diesel generator that weighs about 170kg. The climbers rig up a pulley system but a rope protector – a tough fabric sheath to stop climbing ropes fraying on sharp edges – gets caught in a pulley jamming the whole thing up and leaving the machine dangling over water. Anthony attaches a ratchet strap and uses it to take the weight allowing the pulley to be freed. The generator is fired up, the projector connected and... nothing, no power. The diesel engine is ticking over fine but there's no electricity coming out. The ship's electrician is sent for.

The Warrior is equipped with chains to enable the crew to lock themselves inside if ever boarded by aggressors and Penny asks me to check they are all ready if needed. Entering the mess, I am confronted by eager faces who have been shut away down here the whole time. I tell them what's happening up top and to stand by.

The tide is falling and the deck of the *Warrior* is almost level with the quay. John is talking to a short bloke wearing safety glasses and an orange hi-viz coat who appears to be in charge of the dock. Unfortunately they are standing right where we want to disembark the activists below. Patrick sidles up to John and has a quiet word in his ear. After a minute, John – still talking to the dock manager – slowly walks along the deck, drawing the other along with him. Patrick motions me to put my foot against a plank that had been placed up to the railing to steady it. The main door opens and out pour the thirty, each carrying a flag. Up the plank and a big step over onto the quay. The E.ON guy rushes over but already there are too many and there's nothing he or his mates can do. The last one to walk the plank is the pale faced young woman who tentatively puts one foot in front of the other, slowly inching along the narrow walkway, eyes staring ahead. We're all wondering how long it will take as Patrick jumps onto the rail to support her until she makes it across. John then joins them and they start to walk through the power station. True to expectation, they get about 50 yards before being stopped and so that is where they stay, to bear witness to the pollution both present and planned, with the flags of the nations.

The *Warrior* blocks the arrival of the coal delivery for the rest of the day and the volunteers return to the ship. I am totally exhausted and collapse in my bunk around 9pm.

On the raised foredeck, the projector has been set up running off ship's power and is throwing images of climate change impacts at the power station. The site manager orders a bulldozer to block the beam with its blade, but now it just becomes a screen for the message, "DIRTY E.ON." The manager sends a poor guy out with a torch to try to dim the image. When this doesn't work, a spotlight is sent for.

Around midnight, a "geezer" in blue jeans and leather jacket, turns up demanding to see "the guv'nor." He is bearing a High Court injunction.

'I'm the Bailiff, where's yer guv'nor?'

I am dimly aware of some movement after midnight and when I am woken at 7.30am for my watch, I find we are somewhere different. The injunction delivered overnight forced us to move away, so now we are anchored further along the estuary. The first thing I notice is the ship is heeling right over. A storm is blowing up with a strong wind coming across our beam. The First Officer keeps checking the ship's position as the anchor is struggling to hold with a new tide pulling us over at an angle, towards a sand bar. Icy sleet stings our hands and faces as we bring the inflatables alongside to secure them. Mike gets up and decides to move further up the River

Thames in search of shelter. He finds a spot at Higham Bight. It's opposite Tilbury, coal-fired, Power Station.

In the early morning light, heavy clouds rush over us depositing their burden on Essex. We gather in the warm of the bridge, where we listen to London VTS (Vessel Traffic Service) over the radio announcing, *"There is a 50-metre exclusion zone around Tilbury Power Station for all vessels."* Hmmm, I wonder why?

The Red Carpet

COP 15, the climate talks in Copenhagen, billed as the last, best hope for the climate, are due to start in early December 2009. Anthony has been asked by Don, an international logistics co-ordinator, to help with an action being planned for the conference, but Patrick is asking him to help with something in Belgium first.
  'Why me?' Ant asks.
  'Because, Anthony my friend,' Patrick says, 'you look like a policeman.'
  'Well, I was going to Copenhagen, I could perhaps squeeze this in first.'
  'Good, do you own a dark suit?'
  'My doorman's outfit is black.' Ant had been working as a bouncer through the winter.
  'Bring it. Meet Tom at St Pancras and take the Eurostar to Brussels, I'll see you there.'

When Ant meets Tom, they conclude they could both pass as police and wonder what's in store for them. Patrick picks them up from the railway station and takes them for a tour of Brussels including a stroll past the Justus Lipsius building, home to the European Council.
  'See them cameras.' Patrick nods at the CCTV mounted on the walls. 'Facial recognition, that's why I'm here. Leon, the Belgium co-ordinator, is on their database.'
  Tom and Ant exchange nervous glances.
  'So this is where it, whatever it is, is happening?' Ant asks.
  'Yeah, wicked plan though. I'll tell you later.'

They drive over to the Ghent Warehouse. Parked outside are two big black cars and a grey minivan. Leon is there and explains the idea has been borrowed from an Australian stunt show where they try to smuggle an actor dressed as Osama Bin Laden into a big security conference.

'In two days time,' Leon says, getting out of the Mercedes. 'There will be a big EU summit and we're going to gatecrash it. These vehicles have been fitted with flashing blue lights behind the grills so they look like police.'

'I think we should take them out for a spin,' Patrick says. 'Practice travelling in close formation.'

'With the blue lights on?' Ant asks.

'Yeah, why not.'

'This is very illegal,' Leon says.

'We have to get it right so we do need to practice,' Patrick says, 'and it'll be fun.'

It is indeed fun. Ant drives one car and Tom the other, with the van sandwiched in the middle, they drive together around Ghent, once without blue lights and once with, looking very much like a high profile motorcade.

Back at the warehouse, the twelve activists taking part are given a legal briefing in a meeting room. It's a multinational team, from Belgium, France, Germany, UK and Monaco. They will almost certainly be arrested and the offences serious, so are given the chance to back out. Everyone understands the risks and that it's an individual's choice whether to go through with it. A couple of them are wobbling.

Ant speaks up, 'We have to do this. Now is the time. The EU are major players at COP and if the talks fail, we're all going to burn.'

They discuss the plan further and eventually all agree that the action needs to go ahead. Patrick tells Ant and Tom to get their hair cut, tonight.

'You have to look the part,' he says.

The next morning, they dress in their dark suits and prepare the vehicles. Each one has a fake pass attached to the windscreen an-

27

nouncing them as The People's Republic of Macronesia. Ant gets behind the wheel of a top of the range Peugeot saloon and runs his hands over the leather, savouring the new, luxury car smell. Once his passengers join him and they get on the road with the heating on, aftershave and deodorant take over. Ben is driving the other car and Tom, the Mercedes minivan. When they get to Brussels, they park up at the holding point. Patrick is watching the EU building from a coffee shop and Leon is in a hotel room overlooking.

They are all waiting in position. Tom radios Ant.

'Is your car deathly quiet?'

'It is,' Ant replies. He continues, 'What do you do to stop a dog shagging your leg?'

'Err, go ahead.'

'Pick it up and give it a blow job.'

Ant's car erupts with laughter breaking the tension but in Tom's van it goes down leaden.

An hour passes. Patrick reports that media are lined up at the entrance and Leon can see the delegates starting to arrive. The instruction is given. "Go, go, go." The vehicles set off on their route which takes them to the back of the queue of arriving officials. All the other cars have their blue lights flashing, so the Greenpeace convoy keeps theirs on too. As they approach the first security, Ant sets his face, trying not to give away the pounding within his chest. They are waved through and he takes a deep breath as they queue up somewhere between Fredrik Reinfeldt, the Swedish Prime Minister and the UK Prime Minister, Gordon Brown. Ant looks over to the German activist sat next to him.

'You know, I think this is actually going to work.'

They inch forward. Another check point and men with guns. Again they are waved through. There is now just one motorcade ahead of them and Ant can see the red carpet to welcome dignitaries. The car in front pulls away and it's now their turn. Before the minivan even stops, the doors are being opened and it all looks completely professional. The Greenpeace "delegate" hops out and instead of going inside, turns to the world's media and starts reading a statement. Two others unfurl banners saying, "EU: SAVE COPENHAGEN."

Security look at each other, one points at the Greenpeace team and waves at the others to do something. The "delegate" gets to the end of his statement before being tackled.

'...the time to act is n-owwww.'

A guard leans in through Ben's open window and says, 'These people are impostors, get your car out of here!'

'Okay, I go.' Ben wastes no time driving away.

"The Impostors" are arrested and bundled around the corner. There is confusion and they are left to wait there. The German from Ant's car, who is dressed smartly in a cravat, decides to wander off. He walks up to the security barrier, full of Teutonic confidence, looks at the guard and waves his hand indicating to lift it, which the operator does. The German strolls off, never to be seen again.

The others are all taken to the central police station and spend the night in cells.

The next morning Ant is woken early and presented in front of a lawyer who explains he is going straight to court.

At the Court House, he is put into a holding cell and left there for the rest of the day. The only time he sees anyone is when an officer brings him lunch of a Belgium waffle and a bread baton. At around 4pm, he is taken with the other ten activists up to a courtroom where the Judge, slowly shaking his head, says;

'I understand this was a peaceful protest but the matter of the blue lights is serious. We will deal with this at a later date. You are to be released on bail.'

Greenpeace volunteers are going on to the COP15 climate conference, so Ant decides to join them, taking the train to Copenhagen. Almost everyone onboard is going to the talks and there is a festival atmosphere. Banners are draped across windows as activists are joined by performance artists. Singing breaks out amid the banter and for the first leg of the journey, Ant is sharing a compartment with a Greenpeace colleague and an American economics student. They get into a heated debate.

'You still have to fly goods around the world— '

'No you don't,' Ant says.

'Of course you do.' The American raises his hands in frustration.

'How are you going to get fresh asparagus if it's not wrapped in plastic and flown in?'

'You don't, you only get your fresh asparagus when it's in season locally.'

'But that's not how trade works.'

'And that, my friend, is where you are going wrong.'

The American sits back, shaking his head. The concept too alien for him.

The train quietens down around midnight as sleeper compartments are filled but then it stops at a border crossing and police come on-board. They walk through, checking passports and decide to arrest the only black man on the train. The carriage is packed with middle class, social justice types so a protest ensues with the police telling them to "Go back to bed, you don't know what this is about."

The next day, the train arrives in Copenhagen and everyone disperses to find somewhere to stay. Greenpeace have arranged accommodation but no alcohol is allowed, so Ant wanders over to the *Rainbow Warrior*, which is berthed nearby, and volunteers to be assistant cook in exchange for a bunk.

A couple of days later he gets a call from Don. Can he hire a car and drive out to a remote location? Ant has to use his mum's credit card and eventually finds the safe house where he meets Don and activists from the Danish office. An electrician is working on three hire cars – fitting blue lights. A Peugeot, a Mercedes and a Range-Rover, all black and brand new. Ant busies himself clearing the snow and giving the cars a wax and polish. They are taking aim at another red carpet event, this time, the Gala Dinner for heads of state hosted by the Queen of Denmark.

While they are preparing the cars, back in Copenhagen, Greenpeace get a call from the Danish security services to tell them there is an area of the city airport not under their control. It is assumed to be a warning of trigger-happy Americans guarding Air Force One. Any ideas to delay the President's departure are dropped.

The evening of the action; Ant is following the procession of sleek motors in his own little hire car. With him is Don as Action Co-ordinator and two campaigners in the back, laptops open, ready to send press releases and pictures. As they enter the city centre, the three cars ahead, with Juan, Nora, Christian and Joris inside, put on their blue lights and peel off to join the queue for the Christiansborg Palace. Ant, Don and the campaigners do laps around Copenhagen, trying not to attract attention, but driving on an action is one of the worst jobs and Ant is becoming paranoid.

Checking his mirror. 'Are we being followed?'
'No, Ant,' Don says. 'No one has any reason to suspect us.'
'I'm sure we passed that police car five minutes ago.'
'Chill, we're not actually doing anything illegal.'
'We are, by association.'
'Well, there is that.'
'Look, do you see that truck towing a mini-digger?' Ant points at the vehicle travelling in the opposite direction. 'They're doing suspicious loops too, I've seen it three times at least. You know, it would be hell of a way to hide a bomb.'
'Shut up, Ant.' Don has the radio to his ear. 'They're about to go in.'

At the red carpet, Juan and Nora, dressed immaculately in a tuxedo and an evening gown are striding inside with Christian shepherding them as a bodyguard. At the entrance, they stop and pull out banners, "POLITICIANS TALK, LEADERS ACT." There is a moment of confusion, then security leap in and bundle them away from the media's attention. Juan, Nora, Christian and Joris, who remained outside, are arrested and whisked off a police station. The three car drivers are taken to a waiting room, from which they simply walk away, leaving the Palace.

Ant and Don drop off the campaigners and go to a pub for some relaxing medication. The following day, one of the campaigners phones Don.

Ant comes out of the bathroom to find Don packing.
'What's up?'
'Pack your bags, we have to go, now,' Don says.
'Why?'
'Gerry, the campaigner, had Interpol turn up at his door this morning. We need to leave the country immediately.'

They jump into the hire car and race north, crossing into Sweden. It's getting late so they find a hotel with a bar and get drunk. Next morning, they drive to Göteborg Airport. Dropping off the Hertz car, Ant remembers that he is on police bail to stay away from all BAA airports after the Southampton action. Don books a flight to Scotland and leaves Ant staring at the departures board. There's one going to Amsterdam in twenty minutes. *That'll do*, he thinks and buys a ticket.

As the plane lifts off, Ant takes a deep breath and grins. The tension falls from his shoulders and he is trying not to laugh. The passenger next to him gives him a quizzical look. Ant starts to giggle. *He hasn't a clue what I've just done.*

The next time Anthony visits Scandanavia, the outcome is very different.

Footnote:
The Red Carpet Four, as they became known as, were detained for 20 days in Fængsel Vestre Prison. Eleven activists eventually went to trial in August 2011, the Red Carpet Four, the two "bodyguards," three drivers and two campaigners. The Copenhagen City Court recognised the peaceful and political nature of the protest but found them guilty of trespass, falsification of documents, and impersonating a public official, and not guilty of having committed an offence against Denmark's Queen. They were given 14 day suspended sentences and Nordic Greenpeace was fined 10,000 Euros.
The COP15 talks are generally regarded as a failure.

Shutting Down Kingsnorth Power Station

"Never doubt that a small group of thoughtful, committed citizens can change the world; indeed, it's the only thing that ever has." – Margaret Mead

It is still very dark as four men load the van with a small inflatable boat and drive through Medway. It's 4am, early October 2007. When they reach the estuary, they realise there is a problem.
'Where's the water?' Sterl asks.
'That's odd, the tide should be in now.'
Dave groans. 'We can't launch in that.' He points at the mud.
'There's a place further down,' Patrick says, 'a sea wall, we'll try that.'

As dawn threatens to break open the day, a minibus pulls up at the front gates of Kingsnorth Power Station. Out jump activists with placards and banners which they drape over the steel fences. They start chanting, "No new coal." A lone guard in a small cubicle inside the perimeter radios through to the main office:
'We have protestors here.'
As security assemble at the main gate, Joss and Terri are with another group of activists, wearing red overalls and yellow hard hats, making their way along the sea wall, until they reach a gate at the rear of the station and entry is gained. Both are young, early twenties. Joss is fair with an easy going manner, he is Greenpeace's coal campaigner. Terri has an attractive round face, framed by dark hair, it's her first action. She hurries to keep up with her buddy, Richie who is experienced and has memorised a map of the site. Joss feels for the phone in his pocket, it will be his job to talk to media

from the front line. He pulls it out and turns it on as they cross an internal road onto a patch of grass. He tucks it under his jumper as it bleeps the wake-up tune. The only other sounds are nervous whispers between them as they find their way to the buildings where the conveyors start. Inside the metal sheds it is dark and everything is coated in black dust. Terri is breathing hard and the grime hits her throat, making her cough. She retrieves the mask she's been given from her small rucksack and pulls it over her face. Richie checks she's alright and then calls out to Luke, the team leader;:

'Has the conveyor been shut down?'

An answer comes back down the line: 'Yes, we found an emergency stop button. You can lock on.'

The activists wrap heavy, square linked chain around their waists and through the conveyor, snapping shut a rectangular padlock to secure themselves.

Terri sits on the belt and draws her finger through the coal dust on the metal frame alongside, it's almost an inch thick.

Emily, Kev, Huw, Will and Ben have been walking for over a mile, they are accompanied by "porters," loaded down with heavy backpacks of everything needed to complete the job. All are experienced activists. Will, the photographer, is the youngest, his eyes hold a boyish innocence. Ben and Emily are in their thirties and work for Greenpeace. Ben, as Communications Manager, has a background in journalism, and Emily is the organisation's Activist Co-ordinator. With a soft New Zealand accent and long dark hair, she radiates energy. They reach a gate in the fencing, tucked around the side of the station, and a padlock is cut off. This is as far as their help can come, from now on the climbers will be carrying the full load, over 50 kgs each. They walk into the compound, gravel crunching under laden feet, then tarmac as they follow a route around the buildings to the chimney that dominates the surrounding countryside. A site worker in a white pick-up truck spots them and races over. Huw goes to speak to him.

'What did you say?' Ben asks on Huw's return.

'I just said we're here to climb the chimney, make sure no one turns the power station on.'

'What did he say?'
'Good luck, be safe.'

Sterl, Patrick, Dave and the van driver are looking over the sea wall. There is water below but it's a ten foot drop.

'This will have to do,' Patrick says. 'Get the boat out.'

They open the van doors and pull the inflatable to the wall. The four of them lift it over and lower it on short ropes. It has to fall the last five foot and as it hits the water, it becomes apparent there are rocks underneath. When they drop themselves into the boat, they find that a rear sponson – one of the inflated chambers – has burst. Water is swilling over the stern where the small outboard motor is attached, drenching their bag of food. Sterl, tall and lean, is breathing heavily, he hasn't let on but two years ago, was diagnosed with chronic fatigue syndrome. Any physical exertion takes it out of him.

'Are we sinking?' Dave asks.

'Nah, it's fine. You two sit on the front, we should be okay,' Patrick replies.

The engine fires and like a bee in a tin can, buzzes them out into the estuary.

The climb team reach the chimney, sagging under their loads. A wide roller-shutter door is gaping open for them. They walk in and dumping bags, Ben presses the button to wind the shutters down, securing the door. But there are other doors, if anyone got in now and seized the equipment before they gained height, it would be game over. Three of the doors can be locked but one remains vulnerable, so a rope is tied to its handle and around a scaffold bar. It's hot inside, four seven metre diameter flues are piping smoke and CO_2 at 120 deg.C. Around the outside, steps lead up to the next floor. Huw is inspecting them:

'We have a problem. The steps only go this far.' He points to the level above him.

'What do you mean?' Ben asks.

'They stop at the first level and from then on it's a vertical ladder.'

'Shit, but we were told—'

'I know. There is a backscratcher,' Huw says, referring to metal rings that make a tubular frame, as a safety measure.

'It'll take hours with all this lot.' Ben points at the pile of bags. 'If it's even possible.'

'I can rig up a system,' Kev says. 'I always carry pulleys in case of emergency.'

'We'll have to try,' Emily says. 'See how we get on. If we can't do it, well...' She forces a smile of resignation.

Sterl, Patrick and Dave have completed their marine approach and are now looking for their target. It's a specific building essential to the power station's back-up operation.

'This is it.' Patrick is pointing through the half-light at a two-story building sitting between massive oil tanks.

The doors are unlocked so they go inside and set to work. They've carried tools, angle iron and coach bolts in rucksacks which are used to secure all the entrances, turning off power to the roller shutter door and screwing the rest shut. There is a metal staircase leading up to the first floor and a mezzanine area overlooking the pumps. Kingsnorth is mainly coal-fired but can also run on oil. To properly shut the plant down, they need to ensure that it cannot be switched over once the coal conveyor is blocked. Having taken over the pumping station, they search the upstairs rooms and discover the operating desk.

Sterl looks at the flashing lights, dials and switches laid out before him. 'Should we—'

'No!' Patrick replies. 'We don't know what'll happen.'

Dave comes in having looked through the other rooms. 'There's a dining area, and a toilet, so we're all set up for a long stay, nice and comfy.'

'Bit short on grub though.' Sterl holds up the sodden food bag.

'There's a telephone.' Patrick points at the desk. 'Perhaps we can get a pizza delivered?' He picks it up and notices the list of internal numbers. He dials one. 'Is that the canteen? . . . Excellent, could you send over three pasties please? . . . We're in the oil pumping station. . . . You don't do deliveries? . . . Maybe just this once you could make an exception? For Greenpeace?' Patrick looks at the phone. 'She hung up, would you believe? Okay, what else do we have here?'

'The dining area has windows overlooking a flat roof and there looks like an emergency exit ladder further along,' Dave says.

'We need to block that some way. Sterl, see if you can get through the window and check out that ladder. Dave, come with me, I have an idea.'

A few minutes later, Sterl is squatting on the edge of the flat roof looking down a metal ladder, with a backscratcher, attached to the wall.

Dave calls to him, 'See if you can do anything with this.' He pushes a heavy metal grill out of the window, it's a section of the internal stairs he and Patrick have removed. Sterl has some rope so he ties it on and suspends the grill over the ladder. Anyone coming up will have to deal with it to get past. When he climbs back inside, Patrick has the dining table on its side.

'Give us a hand with this, we'll use it to barricade the window,' he says.

Over in the chimney, the climbers are making slow progress. Kev, an industrial rope access specialist from the West Country, and Huw, an experienced caver, have rigged up a pulley system to haul the bags up but the higher they go, the harder it's becoming. Their arm muscles have given up so the team tie ropes around their waists and take it in turns to drag each rucksack up a level. Carcinogenic dust is lying several inches deep and is kicked up every time one of them does a lift. Their face masks were lost in a bag on the way up. With a blocked nose, Will is having to breathe through his mouth and dust cakes his teeth as he gasps for air, having just wrestled a 35 kg bag over safety railing running around a central void.

'My God, this must be like giving birth,' he says.

Emily is standing next to him. 'No, Will, it's not.'

Kev, face streaked with sweat through the grime, looks at Ben. 'This heat is too much. Give me cold any day.'

Ben nods. 'Next level, Kev.'

'Yeah, we have a problem there. Nothing to attach the pulley, only a bit of iron with a hole that's too small for a carabiner.'

'Can we wrap a rope around one of the flues?' Ben asks.

'Only the climbing rope is long enough and I really don't want to contaminate it with this dust if we're going to use it later.'

'Have you nothing in your magic bag that will fit through the hole?'

'A Maillon quick link might work.' Kev reaches for his bag. 'I should have one.'

The police and site security, wearing white hard hats and fluorescent yellow coats, have arrived to inspect the activists chained to the conveyor. A senior officer asks them to unlock but gets no response so retires to discuss strategy with the station management. Luke pokes his head out through a gap in the tin roof of the conveyor channel. His red overalls are covered in coal dust and he sucks in the clean, damp air of a dull October morning.

It's nearing midday and Joss has already taken calls from ITV, Kent Online and sent Reuters a photo of Luke but he's aware of a growing personal problem.

He calls over to the team leader, 'I really need to go.'

Luke ducks back inside. 'Go? Go where?'

'Toilet.'

'Can you not—'

Joss is shaking his head.

When activists chain themselves to something and "lock on," what happens to the key is usually left up to the individual. Joss has hidden his in a place he doubts anyone will look and so after a quick rummage, he unlocks himself to go and find a copper.

A little later, local media misread Joss's name and report the first arrest of the day as being a young woman named Jess.

Kev has managed to keep the pulley system working up through the 200 metre chimney. The ascent which should have taken two or three hours has been a nine hour slog. They are dripping with sweat and shaking from exhaustion with just one ladder from the hatch at the top. Will is emailing out pictures through a small window used to change the red light bulbs that run down the outside of the chimney to warn aircraft. Kev climbs the ladder to the hatch and pushes. It's so heavy and rarely used, it moves but doesn't open. He takes a step higher to get better leverage and tries again using his leg and back muscles, it slowly swings open. He pokes his head out into the cool, fresh wind and the relief is instant. He gratefully climbs out, followed by Will, who then films Emily emerging from Dante's imagination.

It's three in the afternoon and as they look down at the coal conveyors below and see their friends who have now moved to the openings of the tin roofs. Emily gives them a wave and the activists below wave back. Some cheer having waited ten hours to see the chimney team appear, but the real emotions were being felt 200 metres up as the five, soot covered climbers, gulp in clean air between shared smiles and allow their aching bodies to rest. The view is incredible, it's a clear day and even the sun makes a guest appearance. Kev notes that from this height, the long wheel base police van right below them is roughly the width of his little fingernail. They still have work to do, Emily starts stirring paint as Huw and Kev rig up climbing ropes. Ben, is on the phone to the local TV station as Will takes photos of the circling police chopper.

In the oil pumping station, Patrick takes a call from the AC.

'You've done a grand job in there, but we're going to pull you out in a bit.'

'Why?' Patrick asks. 'I thought we were planning to stay longer.'

'E.ON are applying for an injunction, once that comes through, we're going to have to leave,' the AC replies.

Sterl and Dave are listening closely.

'Okay, when do you—'

'Wait, wait,' Sterl interrupts. 'I was told we would stay here for a serious amount of time, injunction or no.'

'Yeah, me too,' Dave says.

'Put me on.' Sterl opens his hand to take the phone which Patrick gives him. 'You said this would be a proper action, shut the place down for days. It's the only reason I agreed to do it. I'm already on bail you know.'

'I know Sterl,' the AC says, 'but the decision's been taken. We're ending the action when the injunction comes through.'

'Well we might as well walk out now then.'

'Don't do that, stay put for the time being.'

'Bollocks! Why should we? What's the point if we're going to meekly give up at the first hurdle?'

'Sterl, if you walk out now, you'll never be on one of my actions ever again.'

Sterl tosses the phone to Patrick. 'Fuck him, I'm off.' He turns to the door and then pauses by the instrument panel, hand hovering over the switches.

'No,' Patrick says. 'You might flood the Medway with oil.'

Sterl mumbles through clenched teeth, 'Yeah, you're right,' and walks out.

As the afternoon wears on and with the chimney team in place there is no need for the conveyor occupiers to remain so, after talking with the AC, they remove themselves into police custody.

By six in the evening, Sterl and Dave are sitting in a pub having been arrested, processed and released on bail. Luke and Terri are still waiting in police cells. At roughly the same time, Emily and Kev are preparing to abseil off the top of the chimney. Kev is doing it for his friend and mentor Richard Watson, a dedicated Greenpeace activist who passed away earlier in the year. Emily hasn't been climbing very long, the highest so far being a three storey office, now she is about to step off a 200 metre ledge.

Kev faces her as he checks her harness. 'All set? How are the arms?'

Emily rolls her shoulders. 'Sore, but I'll be alright, nothing's going to stop me doing this.'

Kev smiles. 'Let's do it.'

Will takes a photo of Emily going over the side of the chimney, her face set with grim determination against the backdrop of throat gripping height. A photo can make all the difference. When it moves hearts and changes ideas, it becomes a "mind bomb" (a term coined by the first Greenpeace President, Bob Hunter). The comments on local talk radio and online content about these "do-gooders" are mostly negative at this point, then Will sends the photo over to the media team who immediately put it out online and instantly the comments change.

Kev and Emily descend three metres apart and start painting using rollers with white paint pumped from tanks slung over their shoulders. The plan is to write "GORDON BIN IT," referring to the Prime Minister Gordon Brown's decision on the future of British coal-fired power stations. Kev is measuring the height of each letter by dropping a knotted cord and noting points in the brickwork. Emily is keeping an eye on the spelling as they are both tired and Kev is a touch dyslexic. They are fighting their bodies and gravity to complete each letter, Kev whistles while Emily swears.

They have dropped 70 metres and are halfway through the message with darkness descending and the wind picking up.

Kev shouts over to Emily, 'It's getting dangerous and we're running low on paint.'

'We have to finish the N.'

'Yeah, then we head back. We can finish it tomorrow.'

Emily gives a thumbs-up.

Having finished the first word, "GORDON," Kev and Emily are pulling themselves back up to the top using devices called ascension hand jammers which grip the rope, allowing the climber to pull themselves up. However, Emily is falling behind.

'Are you okay?' Kev calls to her.

'There's something wrong with this bloody hand jammer.' But her words are whipped away on the wind.

'What's wrong?'

'THE HAND JAMMER. It's not working. I'm fucking stuck.' Her head torch goes dark as she pitches her helmeted head against the chimney.

'Don't worry, Emily, we can sort this.' Kev descends a couple of metres and swings himself over to join her. His head torch momentarily illuminates her streaked face.

'How Kev?'

'Well, if we can't fix it, I can carry on to the top and we'll all pull you up.'

'Leave me here on my own?' Emily is glaring at him.

'Or we could both use my jammer but it will be slow going. Let me have a look at the thing.' He takes the device off and fiddles for a couple of minutes. 'Here, try it now.'

It works. Emily pulls herself higher but the break has sapped her strength.

'C'mon, you can do it,' Kev says. 'Huw has the pasta on, I just got a whiff of it.'

'And I've got Paris next weekend,' Emily says. Her jaw clamped tight, she hauls herself upwards.

As Emily reaches the top, she catches the aroma of warming pasta and Will catches her in his arms.

Pasta and salad never tasted so good.

Four of them bed down inside the chimney but Kev prefers to stay on top, in the open, under a makeshift bivvy. When he wakes at daybreak, he embraces the cold. There's been a shower overnight and between his legs is a puddle which he uses to wash his hands and face. The others are surfacing and Huw is resetting the ropes for the next section of lettering.

'That's the strangest nights sleep I've ever had,' Will says. 'I kept waking and realising where I was.'

'Yeah, wasn't very nice in there,' Emily says.

'I was dreaming of cheese sandwiches.'

Emily gives Will a side glance.

Ben's phone is ringing, it's the AC. He walks a few feet away and is nodding, it's a short call.

Returning, Ben gathers them together:

'An injunction has been served. We can't finish the message. We have to go down.'

Kev is sitting in an individual plastic cell in a police truck, hands cuffed behind his back. As he peers out of the darkened glass window, he watches a bailiff strutting about in a police hi-viz and full climbing harness. Kev smiles to himself shaking his head and sits back, making a mental note to go shoulder first into the plastic wall if the driver has to make an emergency stop.

Almost a year on and six people are standing trial for causing criminal damage to the Kingsnorth chimney; Emily, Kev, Huw, Ben, Will and the AC, Tim. GORDON has been painted over at a cost to E.ON of £30,000. Kev reckons he could have got a team to do it for less than £5k, which would have meant the matter being dealt with in a magistrate's court, the team would have pleaded guilty and the case closed. However, E.ON are chasing them for much more and so it goes to Crown Court and it will be up to a jury to decide their fate. But, with a defence of lawful necessity, where it is legal to cause a lesser amount of damage to prevent a greater harm, the Government's energy policy is also on trial.

Kier Starmer was to defend them, but he got a better offer from the Crown Prosecution Service and so Michael Wolkind QC steps in and introduces the six to the jury as:

'The nicest defendants ever to be in a dock at a Crown Court and they are accused of trying to save the planet. This trial is not about knives or muggings, the defendants are goodies not hoodies.' He is a bit of a character and when he says, 'They care about Tuvalu, do you?' Ben puts his hand to his forehead, thinking, *That's it, we're going down.*

Wolkind calls expert witnesses including Dr Geoffrey Meaden, who explains man's influence on the climate, Aqqaluk Lynge, an Inuit leader from Greenland who describes how the climate is already impacting his home and Zac Goldsmith who tells the court:

'By building a coal-power plant in this country, it makes it very much harder to pressure countries like China and India.'

The defendants give their evidence, focussing on their reasons and when jurors are shown pictures of Emily going over the side of the chimney, there are several sharp intakes of breath. Ben refers to *The Stern Report*, which estimated a social cost of £50 per tonne of CO_2, explaining that by shutting the power station down for a day, they stopped the emissions of 20,000 tonnes, saving £1 million.

The star witness is Nasa Director, Professor James Hansen, who describes how the carbon dioxide emitted by Kingsnorth could be responsible for the extinction of 400 species and that humanity itself was in grave peril. Wolkind notices that a lot of the science within the evidence appears to be going over jurors' heads, so he picks out Hansen's references to historical climate change.

'Global temperatures peaked 50 million years ago when India crashed into Asia. Let me make it clear that the crash was not the defendants' fault. Most of them don't drive and, anyway, they all have alibis for that day,' he quips.

Hansen goes on to show the jury the effect of increasing sea levels to their own low lying area of Kent. That gets their attention. The court is basically being given a crash course on climate change from some of the most knowledgeable and passionate people on the planet.

John Price for the prosecution admits that in certain circumstances, it is legal to damage property in order to protect property, but there has to be limits and the defendants crossed a line. He argues that they are guilty of criminal damage for the very simple and mundane reason that they broke the law.

On the sixth day of the trial, His Honour Judge Caddick starts summing up, saying that this country has a history of accommodating protests but it did not extend to breaking the law. He tells the jury they must decide whether the boundary line presented by lawful excuse had been crossed. He confirmed that damage to property could include damage arising from floods, fires and global warming and that it was irrelevant whether the defendants' beliefs of property being in immediate need of protection and that their actions were reasonable, were justified as long as they were firmly believed.

Day seven and the judge completes his summary reminding the jury of the expert witness testimonies, that carbon dioxide is having an irreversible and immediate effect on the climate and, if the concentration of CO_2 in the atmosphere reaches 450 parts per million, "we are effectively lost."

The jury retires, but by the end of the day, they announce they cannot reach a unanimous decision.

The jury file back into the courtroom on day eight, having thrashed out a majority decision. There is a very real chance that a guilty verdict could lead to prison for the six defendants. All of them are leaning forward, waiting for the Foreman to utter the first syllable which would indicate guilty or not.

Ben has his fingers crossed behind his back. Kev feels like he might have a heart attack while Will has so much adrenaline, he is having trouble keeping still. Emily is standing bolt upright and Huw is chewing his knuckle. Tim, stony-faced and pale.

'Has a majority decision been reached?' the Foreman is asked.

'It has,' he replies. 'We find the defendants, not –'

Ben yelps, the court erupts, cheering, crying. The six grab each other, the cork of emotion released.

'– guilty.'

Ben exclaims, 'Holy fucking shit.'

Footnote:
Within hours of the trial ending, the Government announced the postponement of its decision on the future of Kingsnorth. Seven months later a new policy was unveiled with the words, "The era of new unabated coal has come to an end." The campaign against Kingsnorth had been a long one, fought by many groups, including a week long 'Climate Camp' and eventually resulted in the Labour government decreeing that any new coal plant would have to have a proportion of carbon capture and storage (CCS). This has proven difficult to develop at scale and would be prohibitively expensive. A fund was set up to help finance development but when the Conservatives were elected, the funding was cut. A carbon limit was then introduced, effectively regulating coal off the system. No new coal fired power stations were ever built in the UK and Kingsnorth is now being demolished.

In 2017, the UK and Canada set up the Powering Past Coal Alliance, which now has 104 countries, cities, regions and organisations, with the aim of phasing out coal fired power stations globally.

Source Material:
Interviews with Joss Garman, Kev Drake, Sterl & 'Terri'.
The film, 'A Time Comes' by Nick Broomfield and online blogs – Bex Sumner & Ben Stewart

No Dash for Gas

October 2012, the environmental movement is in some disarray. The Copenhagen climate talks have failed. After intense campaigning against coal, successive Climate Camps, and infiltration by the undercover cop, Mark Kennedy leading to the arrest of 113 activists, people are exhausted or burnt out. Then the coalition (Con/Lib Dem) government announces the building of 20 new gas-fired power stations labelled the *New Dash for Gas*. At the same time, energy companies are experimenting with fracking for the gas to supply the new power stations.

The first of these power stations, West Burton B, near Gainsborough in Nottinghamshire, is nearing completion with the turbines being intermittently fired up for trials. A group of activists decide that this is no way to solve the climate crisis. Gas might be cleaner than coal but it is still emitting huge amounts of CO2 while wind and solar are far better options. Something needs to be done.

They are in a field, early morning, still dark. Danny looks around, to his left and right are the people he spent last night with, talking through the plan, checking the equipment, not getting much sleep. Ahead are the lights of the power station, the chimneys picked out with red warning beacons. Loaded down with climbing harnesses, rucksacks of food and sleeping bags, they walk on in hushed anticipation.

Danny is a freelance carbon analyst, researcher and performance poet in his early thirties. His dark brown hair rests neatly on top of his wire-frame glasses. He has been involved with a few actions before but invading a power station is a step up for him, his heart is pounding.

Nearing the perimeter now and they hear the sound of an engine. They stop, crouch down. Suddenly lights are upon them, they freeze as a van pulls up and two security guards jump out. All the activists hit the ground, like prisoners trying to escape the searchlights, only they are trying to break in, they lie in the grass. The guards look down at them, they look up at the guards. Neither side knows quite what to do. Eventually the activists stand up, turn around and shuffle away.

They regroup in some bushes.

'Well, that's it then. We've been rumbled.'

'What do we do now?' Danny asks.

'They know we're here. They'll be on the phone to the police, soon the place will be surrounded.'

'Best thing we can do is try to get away. Get back home without being nicked.'

Around the circle, heads are nodding. Then someone quietly says: 'There's only two of them *now*.'

Danny is looking around trying to pick out expressions in the gloom. 'You mean, just go for it?'

'We've come this far, if we all run at it, some might get through.'

Over by the security van, one guard is standing swinging a torch while the other is getting out of the passenger side.

'I've radioed it through. The office reckons they'll be heading for the coal power station up the road. Security is going over there now.'

'Shall we stay here or follow them?'

'We'll try to keep— what the fuck!'

Twenty-one activists appear from the undergrowth and are running past them.

'Better get back on the radio.'

Danny is running, breathing hard and trying to stop the heavy rucksack on his back from toppling him over. He knows where he is going. One of the things that hadn't yet been completed on this new plant was the perimeter fence. They all pile through the gap and into the power station.

There's no one around, the place looks deserted. They head for the twin chimneys, six start climbing one and ten go to the other.

The rest remain on the ground to tell anyone who shows up that they should not turn the turbines on.

After climbing 80 m of vertical ladders, Danny reaches the top. A steel grid platform circles the chimney, this is where they hope to stay for as long as the food lasts and they have a lot of food.

After months of secret planning, the uncertainty of infiltration, the tension of the night before and finally the dash for the chimney top, they have made it.

Everyone is grinning.

'Yes, we've done it. We're back,' someone exclaims. 'Reclaim the Power.'

Danny hears the whoops of relief from the other chimney and someone shouts, 'Fuck you Mark Kennedy.' Joining in the chorus, he defiantly sticks a middle finger in the air.

The euphoria is brief, they have work to do. Securing the ladders and tying safety lines. Climbers are rigging a platform inside in the chimney which they take turns to abseil down to. Photos are taken and put online to ensure the power station operators don't try to turn on the turbines. Another team is building a shelter to keep the late October wind and rain at bay. Someone is making a charging station for their phones from shards of broken solar panels. Danny stands watching the activity, then looks down through the grid to the gathering police below and wished he hadn't. He isn't the most practical and hasn't a job to do so he thinks, *I know, I'll write a poem!*

Later that evening as they huddle under the blue tarps, he reads it to his captive audience.

GAS

[Sniff sniff] Do you smell gas?

Seeping through the cracks, of our energy policy

We're eighty metres high, and we feel closer to reality

Than back-scratching bureaucrats' cheap gas fantasies

As the North Sea runs dry, it's hooray for Norway!

Hurrah for Qatar! Jumping to the pumps to supply

A twitching Great Britain, with its hot, gassy high.

Meanwhile, outside the power station, we hide in vegetation.
As security guards go by
And despite being about as well hidden
As the Government's pro-corporate agenda (i.e. not very)
We somehow get past, and then run as fast
As a Tory MP towards a glass of fine, dry sherry.
We dash
For the gas
Through the fence's, massive gap
Hare over to the stairs, and there
Our mad scramble becomes even madder
As we haul ourselves up sixty metres of ladder
Out of reach of security
Out of reach of doubt and futility
High above the feeling, that we can't change anything
Higher than a kite, as high as you like
Almost as high as EDF's latest price hike
And as the gas turbine winds and grinds its way down into silence
In the resulting hush
It dawns on us all that the most powerful thing in this station now
Is us.

But why be so mean and so cruel?
Surely gas is the *clean* fossil fuel?
Yes, "natural gas!"
Natural as an oil spill or a coal pile, natural as the PR pro's rosy smile
Gas is almost as filthy as its fossil fuel friends, it's just got a bit more style
Shoving its way in to a Government love-in
Sinister ministers huddled round the gas ring

Going into raptures over dreams of "carbon capture"
And hot profits from shale that simply can't fail
Don't these fracking people ever learn?
"Would you like your apocalypse on maximum heat
Or more of a slow burn?"

Meanwhile, outside the fossil-fried corridors of carbon power
When the public are asked "Would you like to have gas?"
The answer this brings is "We'd rather have wind."
It's this plain common sense that we brought through the fence
Dragged up the ladders and round the stairwells
To the top of the chimneys, to stand there and yell:
"Hey there UK! Bloody hell.
Our time's nearly gone, didn't you notice the smell?
You left the gas on."

Danny Chivers - 2012

The night passes uneventfully. No eviction team, the police seem content to wait for the activists to (a) get bored, (b) get cold and miserable, (c) run out of food. They have plenty of food.

The next day and they wake to a bright and breezy morning. Some have slept okay, for others it's been tricky but most have grabbed some rest. As they check in with the other group, some are thinking about linking the chimneys. If a thin string could be passed over, then a strong climbing rope attached, people could actually zip-line between the two. This had always been the plan and from rucksacks, kites and a model helicopter appear.

A length of string is attached to the helicopter but the wind is still quite strong. It takes off and hovers uncertainly between the chimneys. Slowly it fights its way across until a gust whips it out of control and is last seen heading towards the perimeter fence. Kites are deployed but cannot be steered in the right direction. Someone tries flinging the string across but always falls short. Another plan will be needed.

Media attention is starting to pick up so for the rest of the day, Danny is helping with press releases while others give interviews. Police have set up an LED message board to communicate. The five protestors who remained on the ground have been arrested.

After the initial rush and excitement of being up an 80 m chimney, and as the hours drift into days, time starts to slow down. Danny's team are sitting in a circle under a blue, plastic, flapping tarp.

'So annoying that we can't get a line across,' says Eva.

'There's still one way, for someone fast on their feet,' says Al.

'You mean, go down and run across?' asks Danny.

Al nods. 'Whoever goes will get nicked, for sure. Any volunteers?'

Nobody wants to leave just yet. Slowly one hand is raised, joined by another.

'I think there should be two of us,' says the woman. 'To make sure.'

It's agreed and a phone call to the other side confirms arrangements. As the two go down, the ropes are readied with quick clip carabiners on the ends.

The two activists are near the bottom and the police close in to make arrests. There would be a small window of opportunity. As they reach the bottom, the rope is unfurled hitting the ground beside them, one picks it up and runs, the other blocks. Simultaneously, another rope from the other chimney is dropped just in time to be caught and carabiners clipped together. The rope is hauled back up, out of reach of the police who quickly arrest the couple below.

A strong line is then secured across the gap. A brave activist with a lot of climbing experience, takes a deep breath and clips onto the rope. Pulling themselves out into the void and over to the opposite chimney. Incredible pictures are sent out and used by the BBC and ITV. Supplies and people are transferred.

Danny is leaning on the guard rail, watching the police below when a particularly strong gust of wind takes his super warm, fluffy hat from his head. All he can do is follow its progress to the ground where it is retrieved by an officer. Everyone shouts down, 'PUT IT ON.' But he doesn't.

After five days, it is agreed the majority would come down, enabling a small team to occupy one chimney, stretching out the protest to a full week. The last two eventually come down having kept the power station off-line for almost eight days.

All are charged with aggravated trespass which carries a maximum sentence of three months in prison, although this is considered very unlikely. EDF, the power station owners, don't consider this is enough.

Four months later, Danny is getting ready to go to an art gallery in Birmingham with his partner and her parents. He opens a solicitor's letter revealing that EDF are suing them for damages amounting to £5 million. He spends the rest of the day, pretending to look at art with his guts through the floor and his mind doing somersaults of panic.

This tactic hadn't been used in the UK by large corporations since the McLibel case in 1990's which lasted a decade and brought significant bad publicity to the fast food chain.

The activists had been a little disappointed by the media coverage of the protest but when the press release goes out about the lawsuit, the phone starts ringing. EDF are effectively pointing a £5 million gun at their own foot. A petition is set up. Switchboards and Facebook feeds are jammed with complaints. Campaigners interrupt an EDF recruitment event with a song and dance routine about the lawsuit. Hundreds of people pledge to take action at EDF's flagship energy conference. Customers threaten to switch suppliers and a website (EDFoff) is set up to help them do it. In just three weeks the petition gets 64,000 signatures.

EDF lawyers are asking for a meeting. They suggest a deal, if all the activists agree to never again trespass on one of their power stations, they would drop the claim for damages. This is accepted.

Danny is chatting to his partner Jess with a mug of tea in his hand, sitting at the kitchen table.

'This feels like a victory for people power. It shows there is public support for direct action. It's as if every one of those 64,000 were up that chimney with us.' There is a catch in his voice. 'We couldn't have done it without them. Without that support, we would have been screwed.'

'There's a lesson to be learnt.'

'Hopefully it will be a very long time before a company tries that again.'

Footnote:
With the determined campaigning against and failure of fracking in the UK, and the success of renewables, especially offshore wind power, the *New Dash for Gas* was quietly shelved with only one other gas-fired power station being built in the UK since West Burton. The power of campaigning to question contentious policies should not be understated.

Danny was convicted of aggravated trespass and received 200 hours community service. During the court proceedings, the prosecution submitted a list of items confiscated from the protest and highlighted in red were the things that would not be returned as they were deemed, "vital to the commission of crime," and so needed to be permanently confiscated. On the red list between climbing harnesses and sleeping bags was; "A poem about gas".

Plane Stupid

I remember the Officer's words, 'I'm arresting you for...' but despite desperately trying to focus on the rest of what he was saying, I don't remember it.

I was in turmoil, my head spinning, hydraulic jaws are closing on the D-lock around my neck. A sharp crack just behind my ear as they break through.

This was the first time I had ever got into trouble, I am naturally a law-abiding, well-behaved person. Perhaps I should say "used to be." However, in this instance my conscience dictated I had to do more than politely sit by while we trash the planet.

My letters to MPs and Ministers received polite replies but were ultimately ignored.

Governments do listen to people, they also listen to Industry and Industry was telling them that people want cheap flights, so how do you convey the messages about consequences, how do you bring ethics into business models?

A year or so before, I had joined a local Greenpeace group and began a personal journey which started with me wanting to do more for the environment, through to the realisation that if we don't do something now, we're screwed (we being a generalisation of life on Earth).

At this point, I passionately believed I had to do everything I could, it was my moral duty, indeed I still do, but all the letter writing, the on-street campaigning and talking to people, was not achieving the impact needed.

With similarly frustrated friends, we discussed taking non-violent direct action.

Being a small group living on the South Coast of England, we decided we could achieve most impact by targeting Southampton Airport and contacted Plane Stupid, a loose collective of experienced activists who focussed on aviation emissions with creative direct actions. Two years previously, they recruited a Baptist Minister and shut down East Midlands Airport by holding a service on the runway.

The big question for us was, how far do we go?

Do we occupy a runway, grounding flights, were we prepared to get arrested or do we simply stand outside an airport waving banners?

After several meetings in a friend's house, a core of five people emerged who were prepared to be arrested; myself and my girlfriend, Janet, Andrew, Sophie and Tara. It is an unfortunate reality of this World that the media only really gets interested if someone is playing up. No one wants to know unless you are locked on and the Police have cordoned you off.

About this time a report was released predicting 200 million climate refugees by 2050.

Shocked by this, and knowing aviation's responsibility, we wondered if we could tie the issues together with something creative, unique. I remembered something someone had said to me at a Greenpeace skill-share a couple of months back. "You don't need to be the land owner to apply for planning permission."

'How about,' I said, as we sat around Sofie's kitchen table, 'we put in an application to the council to change the use of the airport to a climate refugee camp?'

'That's it!' Andrew said. 'That's the hook for the media.'

'We can even help get things started by setting up a few tents outside the Terminal.'

It was going to be more of a stunt than we would have liked but at least we should be able to get the message out there. So it was decided, but we needed more people.

A month passed during which I met a crazy Welshman called, Anthony on the *Rainbow Warrior II* who was up for mischief. "Anything to fight the Man," he had said.

I contacted a local Southampton group and found two more willing volunteers, Ben and Imogen.

We bought three pop-up tents, lengths of chain, padlocks and bike D-locks. I retrieved an old metal shelf from the skip at work and painted a sign, "CLIMATE REFUGEE CAMP – Planning Applied For."

The same message was scrawled across the tents. We were ready.

The day before, we gathered at Andrew and Sofie's house. He had found an old suitcase and we fitted an armtube inside it made from the core of a half tonne reel of board paper, scavenged from Daler-Rowney. Cutting holes in either side meant two people could feed their arms in and lock themselves together within the suitcase.

Andrew had taken a trip to the airport and had photos, from these we worked out who would do what. We walked through our plan in the front room, who would go where, that sort of thing, so we wouldn't trip over each other on the day. Plane Stupid sent down a representative and someone to video the protest. Our mate, Phil, would be at the airport, ready to take stills. Andrew had a friend who would send out the press release to a long list of media, as soon as we got into position. As usual, the final preparations went on into the night and it was well past midnight before we got to bed.

The day of the action and we were on the morning train.

'Tickets please,' the guard said. 'Southampton Airport, going anywhere nice?'

'Winter break,' someone says.

'What's that?' He is pointing at the metal sign which I've concealed in a zip-up canvas bag.

'My board,' I said, trying not to let my heart escape out my mouth.

'Oh.' He looked a bit puzzled. 'Well, have a good time.' He moved on. I looked out of the window, concentrating on keeping my legs from twitching.

We got off at the airport railway station and hung back to allow other passengers time to clear our way. Janet phoned Phil. He was in position and we walked the short distance to the arrivals entrance.

Blocking the doorway with tents, Sophie and Imogen D-locked their necks together, Anthony chained himself around his waist to a security railing while Ben and Tara settled down with their arms locked into the suitcase tube. Andrew and I threaded bike D-locks through the metal sign and around our necks. We arranged ourselves in a line across the main entrance, meaning passengers had to pick their way through. Janet waited a few feet away, she would speak to the media, if any turned up, and was not arrestable. The Plane Stupid rep took the lock keys and hot-footed it to the council offices with a completed planning application form.

And then... nothing.

For the first time that day, I started to relax and breathed deeply as the winter sun rose over the car park opposite.

Bemused staff wandered out asking us what we were doing, people were having to use the exit further down. A temporary barrier and security guard were positioned inside the door.

The Airport Manager came out to speak to us and I gave her the notification letter, explaining that we were submitting a planning application, which is a legal requirement when you apply for planning permission on someone else's land.

Then the distant wail of sirens and my heart started beating hard again. The police arrived and the circus began.

Photographers from local papers and even a BBC film crew turned up to interview Janet.

Yes, they cordoned us off, passengers had to walk half a lap of the car park to make it to the other door, I'm not sure what they were expecting us to do, but now we were non-conformists, does that make us dangerous? Or did they just want to avoid people seeing us? A lot of the flights from Southampton are domestic so Andrew yelled out to airport customers, "Perfectly good train line here. Trains not planes."

A senior officer arrived and asked us to leave. We apologised and declined, after all, we were locked on without keys. An evidence gathering cop in a more relaxed uniform and a baseball cap walked along the line, filming us.

We had hung a Section 6 of the Criminal Law Act 1977 notice on one of the tents, informing anyone that we were squatting and it would be a criminal offence to enter without invitation. We knew it was unenforceable but it did buy us a little time as head-scratching officers studied the wording and reported back to the station.

Eventually the Protestor Removal Team turned up wearing their civilian clothes. They cheerfully told us that they had just been on a training course and were keen to practice their new skills. Risk assessments were completed and equipment were laid out. Once again, we were asked if we would leave and we refused which brought me back to the hydraulic jaws closing on the lock around my neck and a police officer standing in front of me saying:

'I'm arresting you for...'

Footnote:
Six of us were fined £2,000 in total by magistrates. An extraordinary sum for trying out some camping gear! Part of the evidence presented by the Airport Manager was the letter I gave to her, serving notice of our planning application. This was described as a note saying that we intended to take the airport down. I never had the chance to dispute that, hence this entry in the footnote. Anthony pleaded not guilty in order to present himself at Crown Court where he was given a conditional discharge.

An Activist's Story

"An activist is someone who cannot help but fight for something. That person is usually not motivated by a need for power, or money, or fame, but in fact driven slightly mad by some injustice, some cruelty, some unfairness – so much so that he or she is compelled by some internal moral engine to act to make it better."

— Eve Ensler

Someone said I'd fallen in with a bad lot, advised me not to get involved. But really, is it so bad to act on your moral compass, not to stand idly by when you see something that's clearly wrong? And it had been my decision, my conscience that brought me here today.

Let me tell you where I am. I am standing in a disused warehouse with about 50 other people. People I've never met before. A bitterly cold easterly is playing tunes through the vents and I wrap my arms around my shoulders, pulling on the coat sleeves.

I look at their faces, not long enough to be noticed, but to get a glimpse of their nature. Most are young, most seem to know each other, sharing jokes or memories, gentle movements of feet and small outbreaks of laughter. A couple across from me stand slightly apart and I guess they are like me, newbies. Their faces are serious, they're looking around as I am doing, like lost puppies in a herd of cows.

In walks Patrick. He had met me at the train station and introduced himself as the AC – Action Co-ordinator. He is followed by Emily who has a clipboard.

'Right, listen up,' he barks. 'Firstly, thank you all for coming today.' He looks out of the roller shutter doors to the grey drizzle. 'It's a beautiful day.' Light laughter breaks the tension. 'And we're going to be outside for most of the afternoon so I hope you've all got coats.' This time it's groans. 'But don't worry, the rain should be stopping in an hour, so we'll run through what we're going to be doing, then grab a hot drink and some lunch.'

Emily is setting up a flip chart. She pulls over the cover sheet to reveal a scrawled timetable and everyone leans in to look.

'So,' says Patrick. 'After lunch, at 1.30, we'll start practising. A full briefing will be at 4.30 followed by a legal briefing, then we'll head back to the hotel. Well, I say hotel,' he shares a wry smile before continuing, 'evening meal and early to bed.'

Emily steps up. 'Can I just check that everyone's here?' A roll call from the clipboard. We're missing a Jackie. Not arrived yet. Might be held up on the train.

Patrick resumes, 'So, what the hell are we doing on this industrial estate? We're going to practice running 50 yards, good huh? Getting *two* sets of ladders off *two* cars,' he emphasises the numbers. 'Handing them over a pretend wall, putting them up against the shipping container outside and get all of you up on top in under *five* minutes. The reason is, tomorrow, we're going into central London, to a prominent building and occupying the roof. That container represents a glass, atrium type building and once we're on that, we then have to climb more ladders but we should be fairly safe. And there'll almost certainly be armed police.'

My mouth's gone dry, I recognise the location, the building. I had been looking at it just a couple of weeks ago. 'Oh my...' I mutter under my breath.

Patrick is still talking but my attention is focussed on keeping my legs still. My knees don't feel right, I want to jiggle them but don't want to look like I'm scared or I've pissed myself. I glance around the assembled activists, do they know what I know?

At last we're heading outside, the relief of movement. The drizzle had eased to a fine, wet mist. Now I take in the props. The shipping container, the two cars with ladders on top and a strange, plywood, peak construction with seats hanging over the apex. As we walk to an open shed where a tea urn is steaming, I look over my shoulder for the couple I had spotted earlier. I desperately need to talk to someone. I see them, a tall man in his late twenties and a woman a bit older, not a couple as in together but maybe they know each other. They look friendly so I stop and wait for them.

'Hey,' a voice beside me. 'I'm sure I've seen you from somewhere before, how you doing?' The voice belongs to a man I guess to be in his thirties with long dark hair.

'I'm okay ta. Sorry, I don't recognise you, I'm fairly new to this,' I reply.

'Maybe it's someone else, I get confused with faces. I'm Rowan.'

'Hi, I'm Pete. I've... I've figured out where we're going.'

'Yeah, reckon it's going to be a good one, you'll be fine.'

'You know where we're going then?' I ask.

'No, do you?'

'I'm pretty sure it's the Houses of Parliament.'

Being slightly taller, Rowan lowers his head to look at me in the face. 'Really? Wow! This is going to be so cool.'

'Armed police,' I say, eyebrows raised.

He looks away. 'Yeah, that's a bit of a worry.'

Lunch is some sort of lentil thing, out of a big pan. I get talking to the couple I had meant to speak to earlier. Hannah had done loads of stuff but Josh was the same as me, a complete novice.

We are sitting on pallets, sipping hot tea and the weather is brightening. Hannah agrees with me that it's going to be Parliament, Josh is full of bravado but I suspect it's nerves overcompensating. Emily appears with the flipchart.

'If everyone can gather 'round.' Her accent has a twang of softening Kiwi. 'You are all in teams so if the team leaders can make themselves known and gather your gangs together.'

I look through the melee of heads and spot my name in the group called "Ladders," team leader Michael.

'Who's Michael?' I ask a woman next to me.

'Which one?' she replies.

'Team leader?'

'That will be him, over there.' She points at a tall man several others are already gravitating towards.

There are six of us, including Michael, in "Ladders." We introduce ourselves. It's good to see Rowan there, someone I can talk to.

61

Michael is a tall, studious looking man in his late thirties. 'The cars will pull up,' he says, 'two beeps on the horn, then our job is to take those,' he points at two sets of ladders fixed to car roof racks, 'off and pass them over a low wall.'

'Is that it?' someone asks.

'Essentially yes but timing is critical, that's why we're going to be doing lots of dry runs.'

'What happens after we've got the ladders over the wall?'

'We either run around or jump over the wall, to join the rest. There is a fair drop down the other side.'

We all turn to look at planks that have been laid out on oil drums to represent the wall.

Teams arrange themselves. The two cars drive off around a corner, then speed at a full four mph back into the yard. Two horn parps and we leap uncertainly into action. Other teams come running around the corner. Lots of fumbling, people getting in the way, heads ducking as ladders swing around and are passed over the imaginary wall to waiting hands, whisked away and swung up against the steel cargo container. Calls of "foot that ladder." Activists busy climbing and assembling on top.

We look at each other and saunter over to join the queue.

'I want everyone up there,' shouts Patrick.

Eventually, a little crowded together, we're all standing on the container. The activity has eased the tension in me and I'm good with heights but I sense others are not so relaxed.

Patrick is on the ground looking up at us. 'Good,' he says, 'but that was fifteen minutes, we need to get it down to five. Let's try again.'

As the cars reposition, our team forms a circle. Michael is talking.

'We need to have specific roles here, the ladders are a hazard so I suggest we have two people to stop tourists getting in the way, that leaves two people for each car to undo the roof clamps and take the ladders off.'

'The ladders are quite heavy, can the blockers help pass them over the wall?'

'Yeah, that should work.'

Roles are chosen or assigned, I'm quick with my hands so I'm taking a rear roof clamp off.

The exercise is re-run. This time there is less fumbling, more organised, but it still takes ten minutes.

We do it again, and again.

'We've got to keep at it until we're under five minutes,' insists Patrick, but we don't.

Our last attempt and we're pretty slick but getting a bit weary too. Tummies rumbling, mine especially, the lentils are having an effect. We manage to complete the exercise in six minutes and that will have to be good enough.

We break for tea and briefings and cram inside the cosy shed. Diagrams, photos and lists now line the walls.

Emily tells us what's planned, a campaigner tells us why and Patrick tells us how. It *is* to be the Houses of Parliament.

In two months time, the big climate talks in Copenhagen are due to start. We need to show the government that people feel really strongly about this problem, are willing to take risks and give an impetus to Ed Milliband, the Climate Secretary, who was being sent, on our behalf, to the negotiations. This is 2009, how many years will it take for world leaders to realise the full extent of the climate crisis? How long do they think they can carry on with business-as-usual?

By now my stomach is in full revolt, I worry about some form of explosion.

One last briefing, the legal one. Worst case scenarios are read out and it doesn't make my condition any easier. Trespass on a Special Protected Area, even terrorism acts are mentioned. We are all given the option to back out. No one does. By the time it's over, I'm straight out of there almost jet-powered.

'Give the apex seats a go,' says Patrick. 'You have to do it in pairs to counterbalance each other, it's a bit tricky.'

I look at the construction. Two planks are joined by ropes going over the peak of a makeshift roof, a few feet high. I'm standing next to Rowan.

'You wanna try it out?' he says.

We watch a couple lower themselves into the seats, get it wrong and slide to the ground.

I shake my head. 'I can't see me using that.'

Rowan agrees and then jumps at the chance to have a go.

Hannah comes over.

'What's your job?' I ask.

She smiles. 'I have to stand in front of the armed police and hold a banner in their faces so they know who we are.'

At the thought of machine-gun toting security, my stomach once again hits the floor.

As the autumn sun disappears in a late, after rain, glow, we're bussed off to a Travelodge to grab food, relax, contemplate our fates and, in my case, use the toilet again. After about the third visit, I realise there's going to be a considerable benefit to this "cleansing" for the action tomorrow.

Eventually my head meets a pillow and it's fair buzzing with re-runs of what's expected of us. Every time weariness overcomes me, a devilish little thought about the action pops up to activate a burst of adrenaline and I know I'm not getting to sleep until the hormone subsides.

The next day and I have slept a little. It is Sunday and we are not due to kick off until 3pm so have time for breakfast.

Back on the bus, we have a long trip into London, several hours, and I close my eyes, trying to rest. Tourist style baseball caps and backpacks are issued. Bags loaded with muesili bars, bottled water, ropes and Imodium.

Now going down an escalator towards the tube, the teams have split up and we six ride in silence. Wrapped up in thoughts, chests tight with tension and heads bowed to the city's oppression. The platform smells of diesel and dust. The people around us have no idea what we are about to do.

Rowan pokes fun at one of the huge adverts for a film on the wall opposite. 'You know, I'm always staring at goats.'

A train pulls in and we step into a confessional silence. Doors close with a sound like retching and we count down the stations to the noise of churning tracks. A nod from Michael and we're grabbing bags, ready to depart the curious capsule of strangers.

Back into bright daylight, a breeze propelled by double-deckers and people crowding the pavement. A quick discussion on direction and a time check. We're very early.

We amble down a busy thoroughfare. The sun is out and it's warm for the time of the year. On our right, Westminster Cathedral, we decide to waste a little time and look inside. The cool, calm of the Catholic church washes over me. I move to the back and say a little prayer. Michael is catching my eye, he is eager to move on. As we leave the Cathedral, I find myself walking with Rowan:

'It'll be okay,' I say, 'I lit a candle.' He just smiles back. I'm not sure if it's indulgence or reassurance.

We walk on into Parliament Square and crossing a busy road, make our way to the Palace of Westminster. A glance around reveals groups of apparent tourists, only looking slightly out of place as they're all wearing baseball hats and carrying small backpacks. I spot Hannah and Josh, over the road, attempting to act nonchalant. We gaze at the halls of power, even pretending to take photos on disposable cameras. I notice the drop over the wall to the sunken lawn below is significant, maybe ten foot?

I am thankful my knees have given over shaking but my body still feels like jelly, every motion measured. As I raise my hand to take a picture, it's like I'm watching it under a strobe, short jerky actions. I take a deep breath. There is nothing more to think about, worry about. I am surrounded by people who all know what to do, people I've known for such a short time but already are brothers and sisters. It's just going to happen and I'm going with it. An immense state of calm descends as I cast my immediate future onto the sea of fate, my heart slows and I stare at the gothic architecture.

Michael comes over and in low tones says, 'No police.' I look up at him and glance towards the sentry box at the locked entrance gate. Parliament is due to reconvene tomorrow after the summer break and everything is shut down. Of all the times this building, the centre of the UK government, is unguarded, we've lucked in. I selfishly wonder if my prayer is working, or perhaps it's Gaia lending a little helping hand or maybe something more mundane.

'Cars!' says Michael, louder this time.

We look over and two cars pull up alongside us. Two beeps on the horn and suddenly fifty people spring to life, most running towards a secured barrier, leaping over it and across the grass under the wall. We're well rehearsed, we have the ladders off in a moment and are handing them down to the team ready to receive. That done, we run to the gate and vault over. The ladders are already up and people are climbing. I look up at the wall, now above us, into the shocked faces of Japanese tourists leaning over.

We are last in the queue to climb on to the glass building which forms a security station. Waiting, on the ground, exposed. Surely the police are just around a corner somewhere? Any moment now, they're going to appear and my brief part of the day will be over. But now it's my turn and with relief I mount the ladder.

On top we remember to keep to the steel framework rather than glass panels. We now have everyone up and the ladders are hauled clear. The glass is thick and slightly cloudy, looking down I can see figures moving about underneath us but cannot make out details. Later we find out that we did it all in three minutes.

To some extent we are out of reach now. Josh and I grab a small banner, "CHANGE THE POLITICS, SAVE THE CLIMATE," and stand at the front to show the growing number of cameras and spectators. Looking over my shoulder I watch the ladders being reset against a gable end wall around the top of which, runs a narrow terrace with battlements. As the first person goes up it becomes clear that they don't quite reach the crenellations, but with a height-defying scramble they clamber over. The next person up has to be physically lifted the last couple of feet by the one already there. Only adrenaline will get us up and we have bucket loads of it. Finally I look at Josh and unspoken we fold the banner and head to the base of the ladder.

On reaching the top, I'm slightly alarmed by how far short it is but strong arms reach down and pull me over on to the terrace. We are on the roof, I am standing on the roof of the Houses of Parliament! I look around, trying to take it all in. On the ground, there are so many people staring back, so many cameras pointing. Despite the elation we're all feeling, we refrain from doing dances or fist pumping but line the terrace with our banners looking suitably serious.

One man didn't get up onto the roof. He is in his seventies and really not expecting to get this far – the atrium roof – so doesn't know what to do next. After a while he lowers down a ladder and gives himself up to the waiting coppers.

Climbers have taken a more adventurous route and dripping with carabiners and rope, scale the roof of the main building above us.

There is a door, opening from inside onto the terrace around which are scatterings of cigarette butts from MPs sneaking out for crafty smokes. Using ropes and whatever could be found, it is barricaded but soon there are police on the other side trying to open it. It stays shut.

A meeting is held, they didn't expect to get us all up on the roof and there isn't enough food and water so it's decided some should go down. 20 volunteers, mostly experienced activists who had done roof top occupations before, make the tricky descent down a ladder towards the bare comfort of a police cell.

As darkness approaches, I feel the need to relieve myself but having a bit of a bashful bladder, I think I'll wait until proper dark. I chat to Rowan and Josh about wind farms, living in Welsh woodlands and other aspirational ideas with my legs crossed.

There is renewed banging on the door, more purposeful this time and it becomes clear that the ropes keeping it shut will not hold. A shout goes out, "Clear the terrace." We scramble for the relative safety of the roof apex and someone produces the plank seats although no one wants to use them. The door bursts outwards and police soon appear, surrounding our precarious position. They cannot reach us without numerous assessments and safety harnesses so they wait, and we wait. And that's how it's going to be. Perched along the ridge like a row of wary pigeons. I eat a muesili bar and sip some water.

It's after ten at night, we know the time exactly, we have a very big clock not very far from us. Any sleep will only be gained by using the seats so I buddy up with Ben who is about my size and we ease ourselves onto the short planks. It works, we are balanced so long as neither of us move.

It's almost October and the night is clear and chill. We have bivvy bags of very thin nylon covering us to keep the wind off, but my back is against lead flashing and the cold is fingering its way through me. Ben has a couple of heat pads so I activate one and drop it between my shoulder blades.

Now and again I glance down between my feet and, due to the angle, cannot see the walkway I know to be down there, just the ground, lit up by spotlights, about 100 feet below and my heart skips a beat.

Sleep is nearly impossible so Ben and I talk, all night and I'm so grateful. Time is marked by Big Ben's chimes.

Maybe I have slept a little as morning lightens the sky. I cannot find the heat pad, it must have slipped down and I am numb and dizzy. Eventually the sun reaches the gable end and we all shimmy along the roof to meet it, letting the warmth bring us back to life. We are encouraged to know that in a few hours we will be greeting Members of Parliament returning from their summer holidays. This is why we are here, to say we are watching, the country is watching, in fact the whole damn world is watching, looking for an outcome from the climate talks in December that will change the course of history and deliver hope for life on Earth.

Most of us are quiet now. The rush of yesterday blurred by the weariness of endurance. We know we've done something big, but is it enough?

Around midday, our spirits are lifted by a climate youth group who assemble on the square below to do a flash mob performance for us with a polished song and dance routine. MPs are now arriving and it's fair to say that I'm in some pain. As Parliament is being opened, I find a ledge and an empty water bottle, cover myself in a bivvy bag and try to urinate but by now my bladder has the equivalent of writer's block. No matter how much I wanted to, nothing was forthcoming. I resign myself to discomfort.

It's approaching 6pm, Michael and the other team leaders are talking to the police. We sense some kind of development so when they return from their conference, we gather around, as best we can on a roof apex, to hear the outcome. Our point has been made and we agree to come down off the roof on the condition they allow us to use toilets without delay.

I am much relieved.

We form an orderly queue and one by one are assigned a police officer who takes us through a door into a small tower, carefully led down steep steps and out into the glass atrium below. A quick body search and handcuffs are applied. In the van I sit looking at these cuffs, thinking how ridiculous it is. We are trying to save the world and get treated like dangerous people. Coming up against the wrong side of the law is sobering enough for me to momentarily forget my bladder.

The van pulls away and cameras flash outside, I manage a little wave.

As we walk into the station I ask my arresting officer, 'Can I use the loo now?' My desperation is probably shining from my eyes.

'Follow me,' he says and takes me through to a cell. After 27 hours, even a policeman standing beside me is not going to stop the flow.

The station smells of disinfectant and authority. Police officers dripping with equipment and intimidation stand around waiting to book their charges in. Now it's my turn and I stand like a naughty schoolboy in front of a chest high desk with a senior officer, on a raised dais, looking down at me, his glasses resting on the end of his nose.

'Name, address, date of birth.' My pockets are turned out and contents gingerly placed in a plastic bag. Even my St Christopher, which I've worn for 25 years is removed and put in the bag. I follow it with my eyes.

'Can I make my phone call?' I ask.

'We can call a solicitor for you. Do you want a duty solicitor?'

'No, I want to call this number.' I pull out the bust card I had been given on the bus yesterday. On it is the legal phone line and a reminder not to accept a caution and make no comments.

He takes the card and dials, gives me the handset.

'Hello?' I say.

'Hi, who's that?' says a voice I recognise as Maria, from our local group.

'It's me, Pete, how you doing?'

'Oh, hi Pete, you're the first to get through. Are you okay?'

'Yeah, I think so. I'm at Westminster Police Station.'

'That's good to know, we'll get a solicitor down to you shortly.'

I'm taken through to a cell. The door slams shut and I'm left to my thoughts. Head crammed with stuff to process. I close my eyes and lie on the thin plastic mattress. It's cold and feels like a dystopian fantasy come horribly real.

The shutter in the door slaps open with a face behind.

'Do you want any food, tea, coffee?'

'Yes, please,' I reply. Meals were a little light on the roof. 'Vegetarian and a cup of tea please?'

Microwave chips and baked beans arrive, with a tea, all served in polystyrene with a plastic fork. A few minutes pass. I think about counting the tiles on the wall but don't have the inclination. I notice that anything that's attached inside the cell, like the grill over the embedded camera or the sunken, stainless steel wash station, has rounded off screw heads.

Night has slunk in between the hours of waiting. I'm really quite cold now. There is a button on the wall for communicating and I keep looking at it. Dare I press to ask for a blanket? I am actually worried I might get shouted at, as if it's just for emergencies. I decide it's starting to become an emergency and press the button. Nothing. I wait, then press again.

'Yes?' comes a voice from a submerged speaker.

'Can I have a blanket please?'

'In a minute.'

Every hour an officer opens the shutter to make sure you haven't died in custody.

'Excuse me?' I ask the enquiring eyes. 'Can I have a blanket please?'

'I'll see if I can find one.'

I'm too cold to sleep. I wrap the mattress around my shoulders and sit cross-legged.

The door opens and a different policeman beckons me out.

'I'm going to take your fingerprints and DNA. Just follow me please.'

I trundle after him, lack of sleep and a body full of toxins, I'm not looking my best.

He glances over his shoulder. 'Are you okay?'

'Any chance of a blanket? I think my core temperature has dropped, being on the roof and all.'

'Yeah it was cold last night. We haven't got any blankets left, there are so many of you here, I think they all went to the women.' He looks at me again and I register compassion. 'I can get you a cup of tea?'

'Yes, please.'

A machine with a glass plate and a display attached, this is for fingerprints. A swab around the inside of my mouth. Photographs taken that would never grace a sideboard. A cup of hot tea. It is all a welcome distraction in the middle of a long, dull night.

The morning arrives with even more entertainment. I am taken to be interviewed. Firstly a quick private chat with my solicitor who introduces himself as Gareth.

'How are you?' he asks.

I lean my head to one side. 'Okay, I guess.'

'Good. I presume you'll be giving a "no comment" interview?'

'Yep. I just want to get out of here.'

'Well the good news is that the people before you have all been charged straight after the interview. You'll be given police bail and released fairly soon. The interviews have been a bit odd as there are anti-terrorism officers sitting in.'

'Wonderful,' I say, my shoulders slumping.

'Don't worry, just stick to "no comment" and you'll be fine.'

It's a small room, a little crowded, men in suits mostly, the air is stale and loaded with aftershave. Questions are asked.

I reply, 'No comment,' each time.

The men in suits are looking bored, or hacked off, not sure which.

Soon it's all over. I've signed a sheet of A4 telling me I've been charged for Trespass on a Protected Site under the Serious Organised Crime and Police Act, that I'm not allowed within a delineated area around the Houses of Parliament and I'm shown the door.

Outside and I feel the elation of a nightmare ended. The day is bright, overcast and preparing to rain, but so very bright. A friendly face greets me with a smile.

'Come along, we're all over the road in a café, what can I get you?'

BP or not BP?

2012. The mega oil company, BP is sponsoring The World Shakespeare Festival and Royal Shakespeare Company, meaning that for the first time ever, oil company logos are appearing on Shakespeare plays. BP knows that this helps extend their influence and gives the impression of being a respectable and responsible company. But this may also be its Achilles heel, with many people uncomfortable with their presence, this could be an opportunity to expose BP's dirty side and kick them out of a space where they don't belong.

Inspired by Liberate Tate, who were creating artworks without permission in the Tate art galleries, certain climate activists are mightily offended by this tarnishing of the bard's great work and so set forth to rid the theatres of the oily rogue.

A friend of Danny's, Richard, mentions over a Christmas meal, that he would like to get back into acting. A cunning plan is devised.

Tickets are purchased to the opening of the festival, a performance of the *Tempest* by The Royal Shakespeare Company in Stratford-upon-Avon.

Richard, dressed in a long coat to hide the costume, accompanied by Miranda, move to the side of the stage as the theatre fills up, just moments before the lights go down. Throwing off the coat to reveal doublet, hose and ruff, and popping a feathered cap on his head, he jumps up onto the stage, followed by Miranda holding a picture of the Deepwater Horizon disaster who introduces:

'A short two minute performance.'

Richard addresses the audience.

'What country, friends, is this? Where the words of our most prized poet, can be bought to beautify a patron, so unnatural as British Petroleum?

'Strange association!

'They, who have incensed the seas and shores, from a dark deepwater horizon. Who have unleashed most foul destruction upon far Canada's aged forests. Clawing out the lungs of our sickening earth. Who even now would bespoil the high, white Arctic, in desperate search of more black gold, to make them ever richer.

'These savage villains!

'And yet—

'They wear a painted face of bright green leaves. Mask themselves with sunshine. And with fine deceitful words, they steal into our theatres, and our minds.

'They would have us sleep.

'But this great globe of ours is such stuff as dreams are made on. Most delicate, wondrous, to be nurtured, for our children and theirs beyond. Let not BP turn these dreams to nightmares.

'Fuelling the Future? Thou liest malignant thing! Do we sleep? I find not myself disposed to sleep.

'Let us break their staff that would bewitch us!

'Out damned logo!' Richard tears the BP branding from the programme he's holding.

Miranda steps up.

'We invite you to tear the logo from your programme. Please help us to free the arts from BP. There will be people with buckets to collect these logos after the show. We are the Reclaim Shakespeare Company, we hope you enjoy tonight's show.'

They leave the stage to applause.

Theatre staff escort them to a quiet corner.

'Are you done?'

'Yes,' says Richard. 'We're done.'

'Do... do you want to watch the play?'

'No, I think we'd better leave now.'

'Yes that would be best.'

The Reclaim Shakespeare Company is pleasantly surprised to find that a lot of the audience did, in fact, rip out the logo to hand to them afterwards.

A video of it all is used by *The Guardian* and support rolls in.

'Hmm, this is something worth pursuing,' they muse.

And so the *BP or not BP?* campaign is launched and they do it again, and again, and again, with a different script to suit each play, all within the BP sponsored season and always to applause until one evening when it's Danny's turn to take to the stage.

It's *The Comedy of Errors* at The Roundhouse, and Danny has a huge, purpose-made, cardboard ruff folded neatly under his coat. When he jumps on stage, he whips it out revealing it to be a neat circle of green and yellow – the BP logo, and carefully fixes it around his neck in true Shakespearean fashion.

Dressed in green, as a merrie, gentle patron of the theatre, clutching a book of verse, he encounters the narrator and describes how he loves to support the arts. But this being *A Comedy of Errors*, all about mistaken identity, the narrator turns around and sees Danny again but this time he is covered in oil and laughing. She describes him as:

'A noxious, treach'rous, belching, oily rogue.'

And finishes with, 'Enough! No more! Now is the summer of our discontent. Out, damn logo!'

This time the applause is more muted. Danny wonders if it was their poor acting.

Outside they are handing out flyers to the audience leaving. Danny turns to Jess:

'They're very quiet, do you think we went too far this time?'

'I don't know.' She hands a leaflet to an older gentleman who grimaces at it.

Rather than walk away, he stands for a moment, a hint of a smile creeping in. He leans conspiratorially in to Danny and Jess.

'You know you just gate-crashed a BP staff outing?'

Danny's eyes widen. 'No, really?'

The man breaks into a chuckle. 'A lot of senior management too,' he says walking away.

75

Footnote:
The campaign gathered support from the public, actors and writers. The RSC dropped BP from its plays but continued the sponsored discounted ticket scheme for 16-25 year olds. In 2019 came the high profile resignation of actor Mark Rylance from the theatre company over its continued connections with BP.
Later the same year, The UK Student Climate Network sent an open letter to the R.S.C. signed by youth strike organisers around the country, asking to break from BP or risk a youth boycott.
In response, the R.S.C. issued a statement announcing it would be terminating the BP partnership at the end of 2019, saying:
"Over many months we have listened to a wide and varied range of voices and opinions about our partnership with BP and their support of our £5 ticket scheme for 16 - 25-year olds. This careful and often difficult debate with, amongst others, our Board, staff, our audiences and artists, has highlighted the strength of feeling, especially amongst young people who we would like to benefit from the scheme. Central to our organisational values is that we listen to and respond to the views of young people."

Liberate Tate

Anthony is working in an activist warehouse in North London when he notices a small group talking through plans. He knows one of them, let's call him Tim for now, so he wanders over.

'Looks interesting,' he says.

'Yeah, it's going to be an art installation in the Nude Hall of the Tate Britain.'

'Nude Hall.' Ant nods slowly. 'Never heard of it.'

Tim explains, 'An activist is going in, getting naked and we will pour oil over them. We're calling it, *Human Cost*.'

'Nice... why?'

'BP are partnering the Tate, effectively laundering their image through art sponsorship.'

A woman called Hannah joins in. 'We want to stay there for 87 minutes, one minute for every day that oil leaked into the Gulf of Mexico from BP's Deepwater Horizon rig.'

'Will the activist be male or female?'

'We figure male, so it's not sexualised.'

'Well, if you need any help,' Ant says. 'I'm up for anything, smuggling oil in, whatever.'

'Anything?'

Ant looks around, besides him there are only two other males. He takes a deep breath. 'I guess the nudity, in the Nude Hall, is really important.'

'Key component,' Tim says. 'Draw lots?'

'Yeah, let's do it.'

The three of them stand in a line and Hannah arranges straws in her hand. Ant pulls out the short one.

'Are you okay with this?' Tim asks.

'Yeah, but I don't want my cock all over the internet.'
Tim laughs. 'Don't worry, we can do camera tricks.'

That evening they run through a couple of practices with Ant in his pants. Tim has come up with a suspension of sunflower oil and charcoal, which looks great but they are worried about it going in Ant's ear, so ear plugs are found.

The next day they rendezvous at Tate Britain. A number of Tate employees, not being happy with the galleries association with BP, were members of Liberate Tate and someone had taken in two cans of "oil," hiding them in a cleaning cupboard.

The Nude Hall is bright and airy. Hushed voices echo up to the high vaulted ceiling.

As Ant takes his clothes off he has a quick word with the photographer:

'Can you keep my cock out of it?'

The photographer smiles. 'No problem.'

Naked, Ant lies down in the foetal position, ear plugs in and holding a tissue over his eyes. Two people, dressed entirely in black including veils, step up and start pouring the black mixture. They cover his body and Ant whispers:

'Over me head.'

So it's all over him and he lies there.

Ten minutes pass and Ant starts to feel stiff. Although on a marble floor, it's not too cold, the "oil" mix is surprisingly insulating.

Security arrive and pull a screen across the hall to stop the public seeing the protest.

Staff come to see what's happening, one gives a subtle thumbs up.

Twenty minutes and Ant just wants to stretch his legs but that would cause messy streaks.

Thirty minutes and he calls Tim over;

'I don't think I can do the full 87 minutes.'

'Don't worry, it's one of those things, we've said it's 87 minutes to correspond with the Deepwater disaster and that will be reported.'

Forty minutes pass and Ant thinks that if he doesn't get up now, he won't be able to stand.

A couple of minutes later, he beckons Tim over who has Wellies and overalls ready for him to change into.

Security point Ant to a fire exit saying, 'You can get out this way.' And they are outside. One of the group had booked a Zip car (a city wide, self drive hire scheme), registering a complaint that the car had 'strange black streaks on the back seat.'

Ant jumps in the back but didn't leave any "oil" behind and is whisked away for a very long shower.

That evening the video is broadcast on Channel 4 and the next day a photo of the action is on the front page of the Financial Times, becoming an iconic picture for the environmental movement.

Footnote:
From May 2010 to Nov. 2015, Liberate Tate staged a number of artistic demonstrations including an oil spill at the Tate's summer party, the donation of a 54 foot wind turbine blade and "Birthmark" where people were tattooed in the Turbine Hall with the atmospheric CO_2 levels of their birth year.

In 2016, BP concluded its 26-year-long sponsorship of Tate citing a challenging business environment.

Anthony of the Arctic[1]

The boat rolls over a small wave and I grip the A-frame to steady myself. It's early 2013 and a training weekend for the boat team. I'm standing next to Frank, watching the other RHIB circle preparing to come alongside. The Thames is grey under an ashen sky.

'Hey Frank, are you doing a stint on any of the ships this year?'

Frank puts a hand on my shoulder. 'Yeah, actually I was going to ask you about that. We have something coming up that you might like to be part of.'

'Well, if it's climbing anything, I've been playing around with arboricultural catapults and I can guarantee 45 metres vertical.' These are designed to get a line over high branches for tree surgeons to rig up climbing ropes. I am lying about the 45 metres but having watched YouTube videos, I think it should be possible.

'45 metres? Wow, that could be just what we need, would you be available later this year?'

At this time in my life, I'm right up for some shipboard mischief, so agree to the prospect of adventure, not knowing it will eventually lead me to a cold Russian prison cell.

I order the catapult and when the time comes to leave for Norway, where I will be joining the Greenpeace ship *Arctic Sunrise*, I have all the equipment I need.

I am the only volunteer onboard as we pull out of the port of Kirkeness. We will be running trials to make sure everything works before sailing on into the Pechora Sea.

---

1 The following is a first hand account by Anthony Perrett, retelling his experiences as one of the Greenpeace Arctic 30.

When it becomes clear to Russia that we are going to the oil platform, *Prirazlomnaya*, owned by the state oil company, Gazprom, a Coastguard vessel is deployed to follow us. Frank and I are watching it hold station about 300 metres abeam.

'Do you think they'll board us?'

'They've already done that,' Frank says. 'A couple of months ago, when we were on a research cruise. They said we must leave the Northern Sea Route, even though it's international waters so they had no right.'

'How was their attitude?'

'They were okay, came aboard, had a chat, told us we were, under no circumstances, to go anywhere near the oil platform. All fairly amicable.'

'Is that a little canon on the bow?'

'Yeah,' Frank chuckles, 'for warning shots, but still wouldn't like to be on the receiving end.'

The Coastguard continues to track the *Arctic Sunrise* until we come to the three mile exclusion zone around the platform, then it steams ahead and starts circling.

On the morning of the action, the sea is quite bumpy, which isn't ideal but the decision is made to go ahead. We get everything ready down in the hold so we can't be seen. I'm putting all this gear on, making sure the lifejacket straps are tucked in, equipment going into bags and even my pockets are loaded up. I keep checking things because my mind's going at 100 miles an hour and I can't keep still.

We're ready, we're waiting. I'll be in *Hurricane*, an ageing inflatable, with the third mate driving, a woman called Anne Mie from Denmark. I'm going to be in the bow with my favourite catapult, which has a ratchet and trigger mechanism and although it will be difficult, should be capable of reaching the 42 metre high platform. The plan is to fire the line over part of the heli-deck support structure, transfer to a climbing rope to get climbers up who would then pull on a much stronger line attached to a powerful jet boat which, using a pulley mechanism, would haul a pod up the side of the platform. This will have two people inside, technically making them stowaways and a headache for the Russian operators.

It is just before dawn as the *Hurricane* is launched using a deck crane on the other side of the ship to the coastguard. We hide behind the *Arctic Sunrise* until the four other boats are in the water, all loaded with climbers, equipment, cameras and photographers. Within seconds a wave of icy cold Arctic water breaks over us and down the neck of my (no longer) dry suit. I will need all my dexterity to operate the catapult but already my fingers have turned white and numb, a legacy of hours using a chainsaw.

The boats set off for the platform together, although the *Suzy Q*, which is towing the pod, is soon left behind. As we reach the *Prirazlomnaya*, I can see the steel skirt that surrounds it, set at an angle to deflect sea ice vertically in winter. This is the same place that Kumi Naidoo, then Executive Director of Greenpeace had dangled from the year before. He had been hosed with freezing water and lumps of metal thrown at him but there was no interference from the military.

I take a quick look over my shoulder and can see two Coastguard boats have been launched and are speeding towards us. As I set up the catapult I realise I have to get this right. I won't get many chances and if I miss, I will have let the ship down and the whole action could fail.

I line up my shot, pull down on the elastic straps until the trigger engages, check my aim and release. It misses. I glance back at the boats, they are much closer. I take a deep breath and set the second shot up, pull down again, aim and loose the small weighted bag. It sails over a stanchion, just as I imagined it would. But the bag is stuck. There is too much friction, it's not heavy enough to slide back down. I twang the line, nothing, I twang it harder, again and again and slowly it starts to move, bit by bit, it comes back down to me.

Crusoe is there beside me. 'Fucking hell, you've got it, amazing!'

I attach the 12mm climbing line and haul on the 3mm line to drag it over but my hands are completely frozen with no feeling in them. The friction is making it too hard.

'Argh, I can't do it,' I yell. Crusoe takes the line and starts pulling. He is a gymnast with upper body strength and adrenaline surging through his muscles. The lines find their way over the platform metal work and the 12mm is coming easily down the other side. Despite the pain in my hands, I am grinning madly, we both are.

This is actually happening, we have come to the Arctic, done our job, smashed it!

Then the Coast Guard arrive in their little Avon boats, wearing balaclavas. They look like kids, wildly waving their arms, pointing and shouting at us. One pulls a knife.

'Woah, no need for that, we're peaceful,' I say but he doesn't understand and keeps waving the blade at us so I call to Crusoe, 'Stay away from that dude, he's a fuckin' nutter.'

We move to the other side of the boat and carry on hauling the line but the Russians come around us and reach for it, severing the rope.

So that is it, there is no way we will be able to get another line over with them upon us. However, there are four other Greenpeace boats circling the platform, all with catapults and all trying to get ropes over different sections. The Coastguard only have two small Avons and are dashing between the others shouting, waving knives and stabbing at the inflatables.

We back off a little way as I reload the catapult. Looking up, I spot a loop of thick mooring line only about 25 metres up. I fire at the loop and get it easy. Crusoe quickly hauls the line over and shouts to me, 'I'm going for it.' And he's away, climbing. One of the Coastguard boats races over and as they come around behind us, throw some rope at our propeller which completely fouls it, stalling the engine. All we can do is drift away until I get the chance to lift the engine and cut the rope off. In the meantime, these Russians are shouting and having a right go at us. I have no idea what they're saying. Then one of them notices Anne at the helm and his attitude completely changes.

'Ohh, beautiful,' he calls to her. Amid all the chaos, he starts chatting her up!

Back at the platform, another boat manages to get a line onto Crusoe's rope and Sini clips on but is instantly dunked in the water, which sets her lifejacket off. She starts climbing anyway and gets clear of the water until a Coastguard boat pulls up and grabs her climbing line. She cannot go up or down while they hold onto it.

I clear the propeller and as we come back to the scene, I can hear Sini screaming at the Russians trying to make them understand that she's stuck while they have the rope. We pull up to the platform's steel skirt and the swell is lumping us to and fro. The *Suzy Q* now arrives, after abandoning the pod, to try to rescue Sini. The sea is pushing them up against the side of the Coastguard boat which is much smaller, the Russians are shouting and gesticulating, then a voice comes over the radio, 'I have a gun pointed at my face.'

Anne is trying to get the *Hurricane* away in reverse as shots fire into the water right there in front of us. Everyone backs off but we can still hear Sini's screams. Both her and Crusoe are being hosed down from the platform above and Crusoe's dry suit is filling with Arctic sea water. He is turning hypothermic and the situation is becoming desperate. They have to get the climbers down. Crusoe manages to descend to Sini and they hold onto each other. Between them, they get the Russian to understand the problem, allowing them to come down into his boat waiting below.

The climbers have been arrested and are being taken back to the Coastguard ship so we decide to follow at a distance.

We have video footage of the whole thing and I'm saying to Anne that we must get it back to the *Sunrise*.

'I'm not abandoning our friends,' she says.

'But what can we do? Chasing them isn't going to help.'

She ignores me and keeps on after them.

'That footage is our currency,' I say. 'It's what's going to keep us safe, we should go now.'

I look back to our ship, I guess it must be at least a mile in the distance.

Ahead of us is the Coastguard vessel. As we approach, automatic gunfire opens up, they're shooting over our heads, goodness knows why. Did they think we were going to try and board them?

Anne decides this is enough and turns around. At last we are heading back to the *Sunrise*.

The footage is uploaded via a satellite internet connection. People are either grouped together, retelling events, or sitting quietly in their cabins, trying to come to terms with what happened. Meetings are held to try to figure out what the hell to do next, but we're all thinking about our comrades being held in the Russian ship.

The *Sunrise* is sailing in circles around *Prirazlomnaya* with the Coastguard ship following. There is quite a bit of damage to the boats and equipment so crew keep their minds and hands busy with repairs and maintenance. The radio has been patched through to the PA system and I am down in the hold listening to Dima trying to talk to the Russians when, in broken English, we hear them say, 'Heave to or we will shoot.'

Pete, the Captain issues the order, 'No one to go on deck.'

So we are all inside, watching, through portholes. The canon on the front of the other ship is pointing completely away from us when it fires. We can't see where or even if, a live round has been used but then it fires again. I'm not sure if anyone has thought what to do in this situation, so we carry on around the platform and so do the Russians. After perhaps 20 shots, they give up. A new tactic is required and a small boat bounces over the sea towards us. Coming alongside, the balaclavaed crew try to board us but they have to throw a grapnel hook to clear a five metre freeboard and they can't quite do it, so they scoot off to have a rethink.

With their intentions now clear, I sit down with Kieran to put together a video interview in the media room, stressing that it's not the Russian people we have a problem with but the oil industry.

Food is served in the mess and the First Mate's voice comes over the PA, 'It's a beautiful sunset if anyone's interested.' So I go out onto the helideck and Frank is already there, watching the sun going down behind the distant dark mass of the Coastguard ship.

'Look at that, Frank.' I point to a shape coming out of the bright red sky. 'It's a fucking helicopter. I wonder where they're going?'

We soon realise it's coming for us. It does a lap of the ship then holds position over the helideck, only about 15 metres above us. Frank is standing right under it in a cone of dead air while I'm being pushed back by the downdraft. The balled end of a rope drops and lands beside Frank so he picks it up and throws it over the side. More rope is let out forming a coil on the deck. Men in green uniforms and helmets, denoting Special Forces, carrying guns, rappel down the rope. Frank goes to the nearest and stands right in front of him with his arms in the air. A few of our crew mates join us and we all copy Frank, not sure why, it just seems like the thing to do. It does appear to confuse the Russians for a moment, they had probably never boarded a ship full of peaceful hippies before. They motion for us all to sit but Frank makes a dash for the Bridge. Before he gets there, he is pulled back and thrown to the deck.

Soldiers enter the bridge and take charge. They tell the Captain to, "Make way to Murmansk."

'No, I'm not going to Murmansk.'

'Then we tow you.'

We are herded into the mess and all telephonic and recording devices confiscated. They divide the ship up so we have access to some areas and they patrol the rest. A tow line is attached and slowly we are being dragged to Murmansk.

After searching the ship, the soldiers find our alcohol store and we can smell whisky on the breath of these young men waving guns around. However, the days pass uneventfully with endless games of Scrabble until it breaks down with a full on row. It takes almost a week before we arrive in Murmansk.

The British Consulate is allowed onboard with a phone so I get to speak to my girlfriend back in Wales. No one seems to know what will happen to us, we're expecting to be either detained on the ship or transferred to a police station for a few days.

We are to be interviewed on land and told to pack a bag. I'm thinking, *that's odd*, so I stuff my bag with essentials – pants, socks, books and tobacco.

We transfer to a smaller Russian ship that takes us into the harbour. The port of Murmansk is not a pretty place. The first thing we see is a half-submerged ship, its stern sticking up out of the water at an angle. The dockside is lined with rusting nuclear submarines and moored alongside them is a hulk filled with spent fuel rods. It's not a place tourists tend to put on their bucket list.

Waiting for us at the quayside are several minibuses that look like they were built to last 30 years ago and were determined to prove it. They stink of petrol.

First we are taken to a military base for a night, then onto a police station where I am sharing a cell with Frank. It's a bare room apart from a radio set into the wall. The beds are bare boards and the toilet is a hole in the ground separated by a three foot high wall. The only time I am allowed to smoke is when Frank wants to take a shit, window open and taps running.

It's been a few days now. I'm not a small person and my hips are bruised from sleeping on the boards. We are asked if we have any medical conditions and Frank mentions that his stools have turned black. Unfortunately this is a symptom of Cholera and we are promptly given a weird medical. Tubes and suction cups are attached to me but I refuse to let them take blood. The results come back that we don't have Cholera but I'm struck by the realities of internment in Russia.

We are told to pack our things as we are going to court. In the holding cell, Frank and I are reunited with the others but then the news comes through that we are to be held under investigation for two months. I close my eyes and take a deep breath while Kieran swears and someone else stifles a sob. I look over at Kieran and can't help wondering if he's going to come through this okay.

Back on the minibus, we see the looming bulk of SIZO-1, this is the Murmansk remand centre where we are going to be held. Getting off the bus, I am surrounded by fences and barbed wire. A guard dog is barking at us completing the feeling of a World War Two prison camp. I am with Sini and Anna as we are taken into the building through a maze of arched hallways, the rough render giving the impression of an underground cave. We are separated and strip-searched in dingy cells. Dirt floors, 40 watt bulbs.

After about ten minutes Anna shouts over, 'Do... do you think these are the cells?'

'I fucking hope not,' I reply. 'I've a toilet with no seat and no sink.'

'I have a sink but no toilet.'

Sini says, 'I have no sink and no toilet!'

Anna needs to use my toilet so they open our doors and I wait in the hallway thinking, *this can't be right.*

Turns out these are just holding cells and soon we are taken through to the main building. It is L-shaped, six stories high. In the corner is a basketball court and along the sides are kitchens, offices and a bonfire where all the rubbish is burned. We walk past a small wooden church to a door leading into a corridor where we collect our bedding. In another room we get a cup, a bowl, a spoon and a pair of size seven leather slippers. It's a prison rule that we are not allowed to wear outdoor shoes in the cells. I have size twelve feet.

Next we go to the cells. I don't know if I'm going to be sharing or on my own. I don't know what the other prisoners are like, but I've seen films and visions of being stabbed or beaten up are running through my head. As each person ahead of me is allocated a cell, my heart beats harder. I need to be prepared, I can handle myself but I'm completely out of my depth with this situation. The women seem to be on their own and I hope it will be the same for me. As my turn comes, my fists clench and I register they are cold but clammy. The door opens and the guard says, 'IN.' There are two men already there, Yerik and Konstan, both violent gangsters (possibly). Both leap to their feet as this big Welshman walks in. They are dressed in their black, prison issue hoodies and start talking to me in Russian. They soon figure out that I don't understand a word of it, so Konstan indicates that my bunk is the top left, he is on the bottom left and Yerik is bottom right. I stow my stuff and they make me mashed potato and a cup of black tea.

I'm sitting here, eating their mashed potato, they're looking at me and I don't know how this all works. I'm definitely not giving anyone a blow-job in return if that's expected. I can probably take both these guys, unless they have knives. Stupid thoughts but they are there in my head.

Someone in the cell next door starts shouting and Yerik rushes to the window. He is pulling on a string made of strips of plastic, cut from bags and twisted to form a twine. In comes a sock and in it is a message for me. It's from Dima:

'Hey man, isn't this great,' (NO! I don't speak the language, it's slightly terrifying). *'Just relax, here are the rules: Don't piss or shit when someone is eating. You are obliged to operate the road daily* (the road is like a prison internet linking every cell to all the others via strings slung each night between windows). *Don't trade on the road, if you want something, just ask but don't try to make money from it. Every mes-*

sage that passes through the cell must be recorded in a book. You have to present your charges to your cell mates, (mine is piracy, they are impressed with that, having seen us on TV). *No violence against cell mates or violence will be handed back to you.*

The "road" works all through the night, is taken down during the day, when the guards are around and set up again the next evening by flicking the strings, using sticks made from rolled up newspaper and melted plastic, between neighbouring windows. Up, down, left and right. To get from the South side to the North, a cord made from torn bed sheets, is passed through the plumbing. If there is a problem with a package or message, one of your cell mates yells at the top of their voice to sort it out. As I say, this carries on throughout the night and either you get used to it or don't sleep. It appears that the guards turn a blind eye, possibly because the Prisoners' Union and gang bosses use it to keep order.

As a lifelong sufferer of Irritable Bowel Syndrome, not knowing when a toilet – with paper – will be available throughout this process, is occupying half my conscious thoughts. However the flight/fight response has put my digestive system into reverse and later that evening I sit for a movement only a rabbit would be proud of.
Overnight the window is kept open for the road and a chill draft circulates as the temperature drops. I lie on my bunk, still dressed and bury myself in blankets. I am wearing a trapper style hat with flaps over my eyes and ears and try to sleep through the intermittent shouting. I have survived my first day in the cell, there will be many more and I wonder, just how many there will be.

I am woken by morning inspection. Two of us have to leave the cell and are frisked with our hands against a wall. Inside guards do a quick search, one of them tapping the metal bed frames with a hammer to make sure they haven't been tampered with. Breakfast is a gruel sort of porridge, I pass. My cell mates then go to bed having been up all night manning the road, but I learn that sleeping during the day is against prison rules and I must wake them if the guards come knocking. So it's like I have the cell to myself all morning.

I turn a bucket over, put a towel against the radiator to lean back against as I sit to read a book.

'Dush,' says the prison guard beckoning me. I don't know what to take with me so grab my wash bag and coat to follow him. Inside a secret cuff pocket I've stowed a charm my girlfriend gave me and don't want to leave it behind. I'm taken to a room with a massive steel door at one end, looking like it should open a bank vault or something. There I undress and the mystery door reveals a big shower room. The floor slopes to a central drain and as I step in, my woefully ill fitting slipper slides away from me. I land heavily on my already bruised hips and wail in pain. The guard pokes his head around, smiles and retreats.

The tap in the centre of the room turns on, and it is literally a tap, not a shower head, just a torrent of hot water. For a moment I relax, letting everything wash over me, then a thought barges its way into my head, *is this when I get raped?* I hurriedly soap myself while watching the closed door. I later find out that my worst fear would be highly unlikely due to prevailing homophobia. However, I'm out of there in five minutes flat and back to my cell where the other two stare at me for wasting valuable shower time. I hadn't realised that it only comes around once a week.

Lunch is mashed potato and meat balls. I'm vegetarian. Tomorrow I'm promised fish soup. But vegetables will be delivered once a week. There is food in the cell, mostly mashed potato. For the evening meal I have mashed potato on bread. I have a small allowance to buy things in the prison shop once a week so I order vegetables, tomatoes, cucumber, onions and garlic. There is a shelf near the window where my cell mates store food to keep it cool.

Let me describe the cell. The walls are painted lime green, not a subtle B&Q "Apple Green," more like sixties Datsun. Two bunks either side of the room, four beds. At the head there is a two foot gap to the front wall where bags are stashed and a washing line is strung. At the foot of the bunk there is a desk and a bench fixed to the floor. Above these are two cupboards. In the middle of the far wall is the door and above that, a small TV set on a high shelf, it has four channels. On the other side is the plywood toilet cubicle and a wash basin with a mirror. Tiny fruit flies hover by the bin underneath the sink. Once a week Yerik and Konstan make me sit on my bunk while they clean the cell with disinfectant.

I spend days reading books, lots of books, I usually get through one a day and wonder when I will exhaust the prison library of English language material. Bizarrely, they are mostly crime novels or westerns. Not my usual choice. After a few weeks food parcels start arriving from Greenpeace, luxuries like cheese and chocolate, fresh vegetables and letters from supporters. My girlfriend, Zaharah, is meeting my lawyer in Kirkenes and preparing a special delivery of liquorice, dried fruit and ginger.

For one hour every day we are given the opportunity to go for a walk. I always do but the other two seldom. I am taken to the ground floor and an exercise area of exterior cells with asbestos sheet roof. The Geneva Convention requires these areas to have a view of the sky, so they've smashed holes in the asbestos which lets the weather in. As winter kicks in, these cells turn into slushy ice rinks, littered with cigarette butts. Ten foot breeze block walls topped by wire separate the cells and I find I can shout to other Greenpeace crew who are also out for a walk. Brits will whistle "The Great Escape" tune while other nationals just call out "Sunrise."

One day I'm circling this area, chatting to Dima over the wall. We hear:

'Fuck Greenpeace,' in a heavy Russian accent. 'FUCK GREENPEACE YOU FUCKS.' Dima and I both go quiet. Then there is a long exchange in Russian between the cells.

'Dima, what's going on?' I ask.

Dima translates. 'The gangster boss is also down here. The other guy, the one who was shouting, didn't know this and is shitting himself. The boss says he gave the instruction that the Greenpeace people are not to be touched. The other says he's very sorry, he didn't know the boss was there and the boss says it doesn't matter, he told them not to fuck with us and here he is, fucking with us.'

'Why would the boss do that? Do you think he's a supporter?'

'Maybe, or perhaps the Governor has an arrangement with the Mafia to keep the peace? It wouldn't look good if one of his high-profile prisoners leaves in a body bag.'

91

'Yeah, thanks for that, Dima.'
'Ha! It's good news, isn't it?'

One day I return from my walk to find a plasma screen digital TV has been delivered with 30 channels. I think it has something to do with Konstan but I'm not told. He uses it to play Russian music very loud for the rest of the day. After several days of this, I retreat to my bunk and pull the pillow over my head. I think he gets the message and turns it down.

As the other two sleep during the day while I read, it becomes my job to "answer the door," alerting them to guards coming in. So when the door unlocks and opens, I put on my best BBC British voice and say, 'Oh, good afternoon, dear boy, how can I help? I'm sorry Konstan isn't available right now, he's having a nap.' None of them understands me but Konstan and Yerik recognise the difference in tone, that I'm taking the piss and emerge from behind their curtains grinning at me.

Friends and family outside the prison can send in supplies and Konstan, who I suspect did his National Service as a cook, makes us some great salads, very salty but good. On one occasion, he gets a plastic bag delivered which he doesn't open but keeps tucked away. As the evening draws in and the road starts up, he seems especially keen, jumping up every time the small tub with a couple of Asprin in, which acts as a notification of something incoming, rattles, leaving Yerik to doze on his bunk.

I get a message from Kieran:
"I'm very hungry, did you get any meat paste in your package because I could really do with some?"

I find the meat paste and spoon it into a plastic bag to send back.

About half an hour later, around about 11.30pm, I get a message from Phil:

"It's tough in here, my cell mate hates me, it's such hard work. Had the fish soup today and threw it back up. I don't know how long I can do this."

I'm trying to think of something to write in reply, to cheer them up. I take an A4 sheet of paper and fold it in three. The title will be *The Gulag Chronicle* and I set to work composing our internal newspaper.

Konstan opens the mysterious bag, his back shielding it from view and starts making something on the desk. He has a vacuum packed, sponge flan case and he chuckles to himself as he squeezes out a tub of sweet condensed milk into it. He has fruit too, grapes, apples and oranges, sliced up and carefully arranged in the thick milk. Another flan case comes out and more condensed milk. He chuckles again and steals a quick glance over at the recumbent Yerik and notices me watching him and puts his finger to his lips. A third flan case appears, more thick condensed milk goes in and this one is topped with grated chocolate. It's about four inches high by now and looks like a gateau. He has made little candles out of matchsticks which go on top, they spell out 29.

At a minute to midnight, Konstan moves the cake into the middle of the table and lights the candles, then puts his foot through Yerik's curtain:

'Yerik, Yerik, vstavay (wake up).'
'Ugh. Kak? Kak? (what?)'
'S dnyom rozhdeniya tebya!
'S dnyom rozhdeniya tebya!
'S dnyom rozhdeniya! S dnyom rozhdeniya!
'S dnyom rozhdeniya tebya!'

Yerik laughs out loud, it's his birthday. He looks at Konstan and takes a moment before thanking him. The whole cake is sliced into thirds and a big piece handed to me in my bowl. As I take a huge mouthful, I look down at Phil and Kieran's messages of misery, *Yeah guys, it's so hard*.

Everyone's experiences in here differ enormously, attitude plays a large part but I can also see that I've been fortunate.

Yerik has seen some of the drawings I've been doing to pass the time and he produces a picture of his wife.

'You make?' he points to my pencil and some paper.
'You want me to draw your missus?'

He nods then brings out a letter and points to it, then he takes an imaginary ring from his finger and throws it to the floor, energetically stamping on it like putting out a fire.

I don't understand why he wants this picture but she is a very good-looking woman so I get on with it. I learn that he married her five months ago in prison while on remand but now that he's been sentenced to seven years, she's ditched him.

Almost all trials in Russia end in convictions and I think Yerik was found guilty of stabbing a security guard. He's not a big guy and soon he will be leaving the protection of this cell that he's shared for eighteen months with Konstan. He starts coming with me on the daily exercise, which is annoying as I quite like this time away from them both. He's clearly worried about the transfer to a penal colony and spends the hour shadow-boxing around the yard or using a pull-up bar, trying to build himself up.

When it comes to Yerik's departure, the friends part with suppressed emotion and clenched fists. Afterwards, Konstan retreats to his bunk and pulls the curtain, sighing deeply.

I take over Yerik's bunk which is a relief from Konstan's cigarette smoke waking me in the night, wafting from below.

Every other week we get a visit from either the British Consul General or his assistant, Josh (name changed for obvious reasons). As I had already consumed the prison library's collection of English material, Josh shares his own books with me. Mostly spy novels as it turns out. I think he is a spy himself or perhaps has aspirations.

We meet in a small room with a row of booths. Today he glances over his shoulder towards the guard as I sit down. He leans in and I automatically lean in too.

'I have a message from Zaharah,' he says, his hand half covering his mouth.

'Go on,' I say.

'She asks, should it be the blue one or the red?'

I know exactly what he's talking about. Just before leaving for the Arctic, my girlfriend, Zaharah and I went on a road trip around the UK, collecting two off road pallet trucks, one blue and one red, for an action being planned for a group called, No Dash for Gas. They plan to deliver a wind turbine blade to blockade a fracking site and need some way to get it in position. The pallet trucks were not as manoeuvrable as hoped so when a green bomb trolley from RAF Lyneham became available I jumped at it.

'The green one,' I reply and give him a little wink.

Josh studies me for a moment then says, 'Okay. I'll tell her.'

I sit back with the realisation that from a Russian prison cell, I'm passing information through a British Assistant Consul General for the organisation of an illegal activity back in the UK. I feel like a real life James Bond.

Zaharah's birthday is the 7th November. At first I was thinking I would be out by then but now we're being told that we will be transferred to Kresty Prison in St Petersburg. Konstan was saying, 'One, two months, you go to big house. One, two months.' So I'm thinking that I'm going to miss her 30th birthday and if I don't give her something, I'm going to be in the shit. I know she's always liked love spoons. A carved wooden spoon that is a traditional Welsh token of love, with hearts and interweaving patterns. There is a shop in Cardiff which has the world's largest and smallest love spoons, which makes me think. Looking around, I find a Greenpeace pen top, which has a wooden clip. I break it off. Using a sharpened staple, a safety pin and a nail file, I start whittling away to create a tiny love spoon. It takes some time but once finished I cushion it in tissue and put it into a matchbox, wrapping that in paper and string to make a perfect little package.

My Russian lawyer doesn't speak a word of English, but she is quite attractive. When I next see her, I sneak her the box telling her it's for Zaharah, but she doesn't understand and shows it to the guard who takes it off her. She talks rapidly to him, he seems to be put out and insists on opening it. When he sees what's inside he says something that must have been along the lines of, "What the hell is this?" This was surely against rules but it's amazing the influence a pretty woman can have over an ugly prison guard. My lawyer smiles at him and says something that persuades him to give it back to her.

A week later, I meet with her again but she is joined by a young man in a dark suit. She has been pulled from my case and this other guy is taking over.

'Hello, Anthony.' He rushes over and shakes my hand. 'I am Sergey, I am your new lawyer,' he says in near perfect English. He has a broad smile and is clearly enjoying himself. I'm thinking, *Oh my God, who's this lunatic?*

'I have the gift for your girlfriend. I will make sure she gets it.' It turns out that he's three years younger than me, a doctor in international human rights law and completed his PhD at the University of Essex.

In the outside world, Greenpeace are mounting a massive campaign around us. There are protests, a giant banner drop at a Gazprom sponsored football match, petitions, national leaders and celebrities are joining the voices of world opinion and even Vladimir Putin acknowledges that piracy is too far-fetched. We learn this charge is being dropped, to be replaced by hooliganism. It's very worrying as a conviction is far more likely. Less than one percent of trials in Russia end in acquittal. The feminist punk rock group, Pussy Riot, were convicted of hooliganism, already serving two years in a prison camp.

We are due to go to St Petersburg and there is a rumour circulating that the prison train is a horrendous journey that can take up to three days, crammed into onboard cells in freezing cold carriages. However, there is a problem. Officials with massive hats keep coming in and pointing to a piece of paper but I refuse to sign it. I've not signed anything up to now, I don't trust them. I've even given them a false address. Then they bring Dima down to my cell.

'Hey man,' he says. 'You have to sign this, it's your release papers.'

'You mean we're being freed?'

'No, it's so they can send us to Kresty. Get your kit together, we're going tomorrow.'

The next day I am marched down to the entrance and the petrol smelling minibus. The rest of the Greenpeace crew are there and it's the first time we've seen each other since entering the prison. I'm struck by how drawn and worn they all look. Their faces narrowed by lack of food but all are smiling at the reunion. Except Phil. He has fought the system the whole time and the system is winning. Even now, he is arguing with a guard, calling him Mr Potato Head and everyone is saying, 'Just get on the bus, Phil.'

We are taken through town to the railway station and a sealed tunnel leads to a train. On board, we are put into cells with a corridor outside, sectioned off with bars. I'm in with Frank.

'Hey Frank, you know, it's my birthday tomorrow.'

'Is it?' He digs down into his pocket. 'In that case, I have a present for you.' He hands me a pill. At some point in prison, Frank had a panic attack and the authorities were giving him industrial strength Valium. I immediately pop the tranquilliser and five minutes later, fall fast asleep.

I am woken by a guard and I am alone. I have been asleep for about 16 hours and now they want to search my stuff again. It's all a bit confusing and I need the loo. When we started the journey, the train toilet was a standard stainless steel unit in a clean cubicle. But it transpires it is the only place anyone could smoke. It is now a butt strewn mess amid a fug of cigarettes. Piss and paper over the floor and an unflushable bowl. When I gratefully exit, I'm taken to a different compartment with Dennis, Cruso and Pete the Captain. There are three beds on each side made from a plastic resin in seventies bathroom brown.

After my mammoth nap, I'm as fresh as a daisy but the others are weary and getting grouty with each other. Not-so-subtle recriminations about who's to blame for our predicament are surfacing.

'The last time the Russians came after me with piracy,' says Pete, a veteran of many Greenpeace campaigns, 'was back in the eighties.' He sits back, the focus of everyone's attention. 'What they were doing was catching whales out in the Bering Sea, dragging them back to shore and cutting them up on the beach. They had all these mink in cages and they would feed them whale meat until they were big enough to kill for fur coats.'

'That's hideous!'

'So you've been through this before?' Cruso is incredulous. He is a carpenter by trade, unfamiliar to this level of public attention. Back home in Switzerland, he would help with the Mountain Rescue as a lead climber.

'No, not like this.' Pete folds his arms and stares at the bars along one side.

'I know how this works,' Denis, the Russian journalist, says spreading his hands. 'We are just pawns in a game.'

'Some game.'

'We put ourselves in it,' Denis says.

'Did we though?'

There are no stops on our journey, which actually takes 36 hours, until we come to a small rural halt just outside St Petersburg. It seems they want to avoid the media who are waiting for us in the city and we are transferred into vans to take us by road. Handcuffed and locked into individual pods, we are driven through the late evening gloom to the entrance of Kresty Prison. With 960 cells, Kresty is one of the biggest prisons in Europe. Built late in the 19th Century, with electric lighting, ventilation and central heating, it was considered the most advanced of its time.

We are taken through a series of underground chambers and lined up in a room that looks like a dungeon. We are all together again and able to swap stories and jokes, keeping up each other's spirits, until I notice the gutter running along the length of the wall, where the red brick vaulted ceiling meets the floor and I imagine that is where the blood would run if they shot us.

One by one, we are asked our name and date of birth as we are issued blankets and kit. When it comes to me, I reveal it's my birthday.

'Happy birthday,' shouts Kruso.

'Happy birthday,' says Denis. This goes right down the line, everyone wishing me a happy birthday.

'How old are you?' someone asks.

'33,' I reply. 'The same age as Jesus when he died.'

We are now taken to our cells. This place is quite different to Murmansk. The prison is built in a cross shape with a central tower and wide corridors. We are all on the ground floor and it soon becomes apparent that there is no *doroga* or road in operation, this will be the start of total isolation from each other. I am standing in front of a heavily built, steel plated door. I don't know what waits for me on the other side. Once again, I am wondering who I will be sharing this cell with, how many there will be and whether it will end up in a fight, hospitalisation or even worse. This ten foot by seven foot space will be my world for possibly the next seven years. The door opens and there is only one other in the cell, he's young, about 20 and quite small. I could definitely take him, I think. Not that I would want to, you understand, just if it came to it. I walk in and introduce myself to Sacha. We shake hands, he offers me a cigarette and tells me that I have the top bunk.

This cell is nicer than Murmansk and I think they have made a special effort for us. It smells of fresh paint and the floor is lino covered. To the left are bunk beds and a coat rack, ahead the window which is upvc double glazed, with bars on the outside. To the right is a fridge with a TV on top, a desk against the wall, wash-basin and toilet cubicle.

'You sleep?' Sacha says. It is the middle of the night.

'I'll give it a go,' I reply. Even though the adrenaline of the last few minutes is only just starting to ebb and I'm now in a confined space with an unfamiliar, convicted criminal, I must have dozed off as I'm woken by the morning inspection. One guard checks the cell while two others take Sacha and me outside.

'Strip,' I am told.

'What?' I look over at Sacha who has taken his shirt off so I do the same. They are looking for bruises, evidence of fighting. Satisfied, they let us back in the cell and move on.

It seems to be quieter in Kresty than Murmansk.

'You play chess?' Sacha asks.

'Yes I do.' So we sit down to a game that I win. For the rest of the day we play, and the days after too, Sacha determined to beat me at least once. He doesn't.

In the afternoon, a guard opens the door and announces "Gulyat" – exercise. I follow Sacha down a corridor, through the prison. We are left on our own, quite different to Murmansk where we wouldn't go anywhere without an armed guard.

'Why no guards?' I ask Sacha.

'Nowhere to go. And if you bad.' He motions a baton swipe.

99

We cross the atrium at the intersection of the four wings and through a doorway that leads to a guard who follows us to an open door to the outside exercise pens. The door is then closed behind us. The yard is about 20 x 25 metres, much bigger than Murmansk and covered in snow. We realise we can play catch inside so the next day we take an orange with us.

After exercise on the second day, I'm taken to the prison psychiatrist. There are a few in the waiting room including Dima.

The doctor, a grey-haired woman in a white lab coat, asks, 'How are you feeling, you okay? You have thoughts maybe of suicide?'

'No,' I reply. 'I do not have thoughts of suicide, but let me tell you this now. If I'm still here, after the expiration date of the two months of pre-trial detention, I'm going to go on hunger strike.'

'Uh?'

'If you hold us, beyond the point which you told us that you would hold us, I'm not going to eat any more food. This is where I'm drawing the line, you go tell your boss that.' I could feel my face flushing.

She looks down at her notes and shifts in her chair. 'Err, okay, but otherwise?'

'Otherwise, I've been treated nothing but professionally.'

I leave her to think about this and Dima goes in. After a while, he comes out and we get a chance to talk.

'Hey, she's really worried about you,' he says.

'Why? I didn't say anything that would worry anyone but the state! I'm sorry but I've had enough, it's me against Putin now. We're here for a reason and that reason hasn't gone away. They are drilling in the Arctic and I'm stuck in here. Eating is the one thing in this fucked up world I still have control over.'

I return to my cell and Sacha has had a delivery from his mum. He had been in a cell of five and she is still sending in food to feed them all. A bag of sausages, a bag of lamb chops and a chicken, all cooked, still warm, the bags are steaming. Prison food is easy to turn your nose up at but this is different. Although I'm vegetarian, I can still appreciate the meat but it's the white potatoes that make my mouth water. Oil massaged with a mother's love and baked to perfection, seasoned with salt and pepper. They are like the best jacket potatoes I've ever eaten. I declare a potential hunger strike and all this wonderful food arrives. It's as if the universe is reaching out to me with different ideas to my own.

In Sacha's previous cell, they would eat all the food on the day it arrived because they didn't have a fridge, but it seems like he was picked to come down to the ground floor and share with this Welsh Greenpeace fella and gets provided with a fridge. So now we can store the meat and take some with us on our exercise hour. You never know who will be in the pen next to you and one day it's Cruso so I call to him over the wall.

'Do you want some lamb chops?'
'You what?'
'Do you want some meat?'
'I don't usually eat much meat.'
'Well, it's here if you want it.'
'Yes please.'

Sacha climbs on to my shoulders and puts the bag of chops on top of the wall. From the other side I can hear Cruso running, a thump against the wall and a hand appears, grabs the bag and disappears. I think his cell will eat well tonight.

My bunk is level with the window sill. Outside this window is another window and between the panes lives a family of rats which we watch and occasionally put bread out through the small top opening. I draw a picture of one looking almost cute and enclose it with a letter to Zaharah.

Hey Babes,

It's Sunday today, which is much the same as any other day here. Although every day is one closer to freedom however long that may be. There's an email system here but I do not know how it works yet, I have asked both the consul and Sergey to find out for me. So on the 24th it will be 2 months of captivity which I think is enough time for the Russian authorities to make a case.

Unfortunately it looks like they are going to ask for another 3 months which I will not accept as reasonable. So this is why I plan on refusing food from the 24th. I will say it is not my intention to starve but to demonstrate my resolve on the issues. I will return home to your arms, in fact I promise I will and I can only hope that this protest will hasten my return.

I understand that there is no obvious diplomatic route out of the situation and I have been assured that Greenpeace and the UK government are doing as much as possible but as you are aware, I am not hopeful. My point of view is unique on the circumstances of the situation and I really do believe that there is very little which can be done from the outside.

Our detainment here is both punishment for speaking out and threat to any others who might take up the mantle of science against greed and ignorance.

I wish I could send you messages of hope from my cell which gets smaller every day but it is difficult to write or do anything amidst my furious uncertainty.

On the lighter side of things my new cell mate is a jolly young chap who insists on doing the cooking! I have just sampled cabbage curry (prison style) and this evening we will be having mixed salad with potatoes. I am probably better off than my ship mates as I hear some of them at walk time complaining about their cell mates drinking all the coffee! If that's the worst complaint though I think we are all doing okay.

I suspect you are suffering the same limbo of uncertainty and I hope it's not unbearable. I have just finished my salad which was lovely but not quite on a par with ours. Harry Potter is on in rusky which I think improves The Deathly Hallows part 1.

There is a family of rats which lives outside our cell window, which some might find worrying but they are actually cute up close and it is interesting to watch their behaviour. The little ones only eat once the big ones have finished. We have made a study using old brown bread but we do keep the window closed in case they get inquisitive as the where this magic bread comes from.

I may be in court tomorrow but as with most things here it is uncertain, I had a shave yesterday just in case. Well, that's about it this end, I haven't been drawing much lately but will try and do something this week. I love you very much Babes and I can't wait to get home, I hope you understand.

I love you always, Your Man in St Petersburg xxxxxxxxxxx

Russian Special Forces draw weapons on Greenpeace activists at Prirazlomnaya oil platform. *Credit © Denis Sinyakov Greenpeace*

Anthony Perrett in a Russian court, St.Petersburg.
Credit © Dmitry Sharomov Greenpeace

Emily hanging off the chimney at Kingsnorth Power Station.
Credit © Will Rose Greenpeace

Credit © Jiri Rezac/Greenpeace

Activists on the roof of the Palace of Westminster.
Credit © Nick Cobbing Greenpeace

The author assisting the female climb team at the Shard.
Credit © David Sandison Greenpeace

Russian Special Forces board the Arctic Sunrise.
Credit © Denis Sinyakov Greenpeace

Occupying the oil platform, Paul B Lloyd Jr.
Credit © Greenpeace

'Human Cost' Liberate Tate. *Credit © Amy Scaife*

Left to right at Southampton Airport: Anthony Perrett, Andrew Butler and Pete Barker. *Credit © Phil Ball*

Despite my cynicism, outside my much reduced world pressure is building. An International Tribunal has met to consider whether Russia acted beyond the law. Every Greenpeace office around the world is organising protests and a petition with over two million signatures, including Angela Merkel, David Cameron and Desmond Tutu, has been submitted. Only months remain before Russia showcases the Winter Olympics in Sochi and there are rumours of an amnesty for some political prisoners.

Vladimir Putin has demonstrated to the Russian people that he would defend their rights in *their* Arctic against these interfering hippies with the iron fist of Russian justice, but he doesn't really want to keep them as they are a complete pain in the arse. A magnanimous gesture to all political prisoners would clear the decks, not just saving face internationally but also gaining popularity points at home.

Greenpeace wants to give him the room to manoeuvre and are not happy about me throwing down the gauntlet of the hunger strike.

There is a knock on the door and in walk a menagerie of high-ranking army officers, complete with giant hats and star emblazoned uniforms. The main man looks around the cell, hands clasped behind his back. He is followed by the prison governor, several other officers and their staff.

'Hello,' the Four Star General says.

'Hello,' I reply.

'You have problem?'

'Er no, no problem.'

He shakes my hand and they all file out again. No explanation, but I later learn that he was the Human Rights Minister come to visit us.

With less than a week before the two month deadline, and the International Tribunal about to give their decision which is looking to be in our favour, we are due back in court. The Investigative Committee are asking for another three months, our lawyers are asking for bail, offering two million Roubles (50,000 Euros) for each of us.

My crewmates are taken in groups of three. Colin is with Katya and Denis and is first into court. The only contact I have with the outside world is through the TV so when I see Colin on the news I ask Sacha what is said.

'Ah, Colin, he, three months, three months.'

My body feels like it's going to fold in on itself. 'For fucks sake!' I had delivered my ultimatum to the prison psychiatrist, now I was going to have to go through with it. I look up to see Katya is now on the screen, standing in the courtroom cage, she is smiling.

'What's going on, Sacha?'

'She go to house.'

'House? Which house?'

'Her house. She go.'

'She's being released? That makes no sense, why are they keeping Colin but letting Katya go? Are they trying to split us up?'

Sacha pulls his shoulders up in an exaggerated shrug.

Denis also gets bail. I can't figure out what's going on, even the guards are giving mixed messages. Are they keeping the foreigners and letting the Russian nationals go? I have been living in a state of constant uncertainty since entering this penal system, almost two months ago and I've learned not to believe anything until it happens but still my mind spins around the confusion.

The days following, there is occasional news of others being bailed but I get sent another package of books, is this telling me something? Our daily games of chess continue until a guard comes to say that I'm in court tomorrow. I decide to construct a message about protecting the Arctic on individual pieces of paper, which I would run through, like a mini flip chart in the pop video style, while standing in the cage.

When my time comes, I have the papers stuffed down my back but as I'm led into the court, there is a ring of police around me with the world's media trying to snap pictures over their shoulders. If I pull out my message now, I'm sure it will be immediately confiscated and it wouldn't play out well to the cameras. Besides I think the judge might be considering giving me bail. As is usual, there is a break when the judge leaves the room to consider their ruling. I suspect what actually is happening is a phone call to the Kremlin to confirm instructions.

The judge returns. Sergey is smiling, he looks over to me and nods. It seems like I've been granted bail but it doesn't seem real. I'm ushered from the court and taken back to my cell. As I sit on my bunk, the guard says something to Sacha and he tells me that I'm leaving tomorrow. All I can do is shake my head. I dare not pack just yet.

'Five minutes, get your things together.'

I've not got a lot of stuff, but what I do have, I pack into my bag or give to Sacha. I'm led from the cell and meet Cruso. We are taken down three long corridors to a room where our confiscated belongings are kept. There is some confusion, they cannot find the paperwork for my wallet and it's taking forever. I'm looking at the door that we will be leaving through, it's just there, almost within reach. They're telling me that I'm going to have to wait until the end of the day to get my wallet.

'Screw the wallet,' I say. 'I'm not waiting for that, get me the fuck out of here.'

'Hey, chill out Ant,' Cruso says. 'It's only until the end of the day.'

'I'm chilled man, I just don't give a toss about my wallet right now.'

They carry on rummaging and eventually they find the paperwork and hand me my wallet. We are taken to the door.

It opens straight onto the pavement and we are thrust into a sea of cameras and journalists. Sergey and a Greenpeace team are waiting for us.

'Are you okay to speak to them?' a press officer asks, nodding at the throng.

I'm aware that I'm grinning maniacally. 'Yeah, I don't mind.'

A journalist calls out, 'Anthony, you're looking very happy.'

'Of course I'm happy, I've just been released from prison.'

We're guided to a waiting car and I jump in the back. Sergey gives me a small bag, inside is a bottle of beer.

That evening, the hotel bar is full of people, the beer is running freely. It's chaotic, people I've never met greet me like life-long friends. I see the others in the smoking area, we have a lot to talk about but Colin's continued detainment is a concern, apparently his judge didn't get the call in time. Phil is also still stuck in Kresty. Ben calls an impromptu meeting.

'The BBC wants to do an interview with someone for *Newsnight*, anyone up for that?'

No one volunteers, they all want to get smashed, but my hand shoots up. 'Yeah I'll do that.'

Ben looks around the room. '*Newsnight* anyone?' I swear he's avoiding my eye.

'I'm up for it,' I say again.

'Okay, Ant, it'll be in your room, I'll let them know. And we need to run through some prep.'

The BBC sets up their equipment which includes a device loaded with sim cards to capture all the local networks and bump up their bandwidth. Probably not legal. I then do a thirty minute interview with Emily Maitlis which gets cut down to five minutes for the show.

Whilst I have been in Russia, my parents had moved to the United States and after seeing the interview, they phone me. They have a right go at me. I'm not sure if it's the combination of months of worry and the effect it was having on them, or what they see as reckless behaviour on my part, but they seem to be really angry about the BBC interview. I cannot be dealing with this, it proper bursts my happy little bubble, it's not the joyful conversation I was expecting. I think it's fair to say that our relationship breaks right there and it will take a long time to mend.

Colin and Phil are released the next week. We still have to stay in St Petersburg under bail conditions. Greenpeace give us a daily allowance and while some spend it in the bar, I prefer to see the sights and pick up some beautiful prints from the museum. Zaharah joins me and for the first three days, we hardly venture outside my room. I've gained a taste for what I call Gulag Salad, which is very finely sliced carrot and chopped garlic soaked in salt water until you have squishy carrot strings, so I make this in my room and avoid the mayhem downstairs. I have to say that I'm struggling to adjust to the change of pace.

In the lobby I notice a lone man in a leather jacket and severe haircut hanging around, playing with an Ipad, taking photos. So we know we are being watched.

After a couple of weeks, things have calmed down and Zaharah has gone back to Wales for work. I remember the No Dash for Gas action is due so I go down to the hotel lounge where the TV is showing world news. I sit beside Ben.

'Have you heard anything about an action in the UK?'

He looks at me for a moment, head slightly cocked. 'No, nothing.'

'Well if you do hear anything, let me know.' I get up and wander back to my room to use the loo.

I return fifteen minutes later and Ben hurries up to me.

'It's just been on the news, No Dash for Gas and the wind turbine blade, how did you know?'

'Oh it's just some thing I put together from my cell you know.'

He scowls then laughs. 'Yeah, of course.'

It's Christmas when the amnesty comes through. Amnesty. It's like saying, "You are forgiven." But we didn't do the crime. There are no cries of jubilation, no fist pumping for our freedom, just a general unease at accepting Putin's generosity. For a while Denis refuses to sign the papers, it's holding up the process for us all and he's under some pressure. Finally, he signs and we can all leave Russia.

We want to get home as soon as possible, flying out is really the only option but I realise landing at Heathrow will look bad. So I decide to go to Paris and then take the Eurostar to London. The other Brits agree and we travel together, along with Po-Paul who is catching a connecting flight back to Canada and Zaharah who has come over for Christmas.

We arrive at Paris, Charles De Gaulle Airport late, it's looking like Po-Paul will miss his flight. But it soon becomes clear that the French don't want us in their country for any longer than necessary. We are taken out of the arrivals queue and ushered through to a train for the Eurostar terminal. Po-Paul's flight is held for him.

We are rushed through customs and, a couple of hours later, pulling into St Pancras Station, London. Ben calls us together, there's a scrum of media waiting for us, 80 maybe 100 journalists.

'Would anyone be prepared to give an interview?'

No one answers. I look around at the others, I felt I had done my bit and even fallen out with my folks over it, but no one else is game. I had planned to get off the rear of the train on my own and try to avoid the circus.

I sigh, 'Yeah okay.'

As we walk from the platform, we are engulfed with cameras and microphones. We pose for photos then Ben steers me to a journalist and the usual questions are asked. 'How does it feel? Were you ever? Do you regret...' But it quickly becomes apparent that something more interesting is happening behind me as the cameras pan away, so I slip through the crowd and meet Luke waiting for me. He has a car and drives me back to the Greenpeace office.

I ask if I can borrow the Land Rover and Zaharah and I drive back to Wales.

As we cross the Bridge dividing the two countries, we pass the sign, "Croeso i Gymru" and arrive at the toll booth. The woman takes the money and pauses for a moment looking at me before handing back the change. She smiles.

'Welcome home,' she says.

Footnote:
The International Tribunal for the Law of the Sea decided the arrest and detainment of the Arctic 30 and their ship was illegal and ordered Russia to pay 5.4 million Euros to the Netherlands under whose flag the *Arctic Sunrise* sails.

Zaharah's Story

Zaharah gave the taxi driver the last of her Norwegian bank notes and stepped out into a cold empty street. Above her head, the hotel's neon sign projected gaudy colours over the fjord where Anthony had sailed from, six weeks ago. She went inside to the warm glow of reception and confirmed her booking. She had used her own name, against advice. The fact she was even here, was against advice.

In her room, she did circuits, examining the typically Scandinavian furniture, waiting for a phone call from Sergey who she had arranged to meet at this hotel. She went to the window and stared into the bleak dusk of an Arctic winter. Looking down, she could just about make out crabs scurrying about on the shoreline between the seaweed and the stones.

He had contacted her through Facebook, claiming to be Anthony's lawyer and that he had something to give her from Ant. Greenpeace were cagey about confirming the lawyer's name and told her not to go as they couldn't ensure her safety, told her not to trust this Sergey who was so keen to meet her.

It was now quite dark outside, why didn't Sergey phone? As she gazed out of the window, the knot in her stomach tightened and she wondered what she had let herself in for.

For weeks, the press had been hounding her for interviews and she'd even had to move out of the house her and Ant shared to avoid them. News of the Arctic 30 was worldwide, with national leaders lending their weight to try to get them released. Of course it would be risky if not foolish to travel to a remote Norwegian town to meet an unknown person claiming to have a gift, but here she was.

Sergey was an hour late. She paced the room a couple of times, it wasn't so big. The décor did nothing to soothe her nerves with striking bold colours and bright blue, vinyl covered chairs. At home, she never worried about being on her own and there was usually someone around, friends or family, but this was a different kind of loneliness, one that started on the inside. She sat on the bed and stared at the phone, something was wrong. A pang of hunger added to her unease inside. She reached for her bag and pulled out a wallet with her remaining few Krona. Things here were much more expensive than at home. Had this all been a mistake? A dangerous and expensive venture?

She pinched the bridge of her nose and stabbed at the phone to wake it up. What was wrong? She went to settings, data roaming; OFF. 'Shit.' She activated it and instantly messages started to come in from Sergey.

'*Are you in Kirkeness, at the hotel yet?*'

'*Where are you? I am in the lobby.*'

'*I have been here 2 hours now, can only wait another half.*'

Zaharah ran from her room, down the hallway and stairs, out into the lobby but it was empty. The restaurant and bar was off to one side and there was a young man in a dark suit sitting on his own. He looked around as she approached.

'Ah, Zaharah?'

'Yes, Sergey?'

'So good to meet you.' His full cheeks widened with a big grin. 'We take a table.' He directed her to a seat beside the window overlooking the dark sea. 'First, I must ask you to switch off your phone and do not give anyone your hotel number.'

'Wow, I feel like I'm in a Bond movie.'

He gave her a quick smile then leaned forward. 'We have to be careful. I dare not give my name here. The Russians, you know? I may have been followed.' He quickly looked around the room. It was quite empty.

Zaharah stiffened in her seat. 'Would they do that?'

Sergey gave a little nod. 'But I can tell you, Anthony is fine, I talked with him yesterday.'

'Is he okay, I mean really?'

'He is doing well, all things considered.'

'Is he eating? He's vegetarian you know.' She reached down into her bag and produced a plastic box. 'I have some treats for him, spiced ginger, garlic, chocolate.'

'Yes, I know he does not eat meat. Don't worry, we have food going in now, but I will give these things to him, I'm sure they will mean a lot.'

'What's his mood like? He's used to being out in the woods, this must be hard.' Zaharah leant forward, searching Sergeys' dark blue eyes for the truth.

'He seems to be in a good mood, he says that he misses you.'

'Can you tell him that I miss him too?' She felt the weight of tears being held back.

'Of course.' He paused for a moment, watching her. 'He has some funny stories too, I must tell you about the birthday cake.'

'Cake in prison? That's more than he gets at home.' They both laughed.

Sergey went on to tell the tale and relay other conversations he had had with Anthony. This was the closest she had felt to her partner, who was in a cell three hours journey east, for over a month. They talked for 35 minutes before Sergey announced that he had to leave.

'And now I have the gift for you.' He reached into his coat pocket and pulled out a small box that had once been carefully wrapped in paper but now looked a little battered.

'I was wondering about this,' Zaharah said.

'It is special I think.' His face flushed a little pinker. 'I look it up on internet, it has a special meaning perhaps?'

'Thank you Sergey. I'll open it upstairs.'

'Of course. Good luck, Zaharah.'

They parted and she went back to her room. She opened the window and leant out, breathing deeply in the chill air. That stupid data roaming thing, two hours she could have spent with Sergey, talking about Anthony, two hours of learning and sharing lost. She closed the window and sat on the bed with the box in front of her.

In a hotel room, in a strange, bleak land, with no money and her love locked up in the same darkness, the same cold night air. On her own but so close to him. She could even smell the prison disinfectant from the box. She started to cry. A gentle weep which wobbled into a laugh and then more sobbing. Since Anthony's detention, she had to be the strong one, the one answering the phone and the questions. Holding the fort while others had the luxury of falling apart. But now it was catching up. Now she had the time and space to let it out. The clutch of suppressed fear and loneliness opened out its cold fingers. She wiped her eyes and opened the box. Inside was a miniature love spoon, carefully carved with intricate curves and designs and a small note from Anthony. As she read his words, all the bottled emotion came wailing out.

The next day, Zaharah felt lighter as she explored the town and found a supermarket with food she could afford. Her phone buzzed an incoming message, it was from Sergey:

'Do you accept?'

'Accept?'

'You can get married in the prison.'

'Ah, bless you Sergey, I don't think it was meant in that way.'

Footnote:
Sergey's internet research had informed him that the giving of love spoons is a Welsh tradition to show love and devotion and may be used as an instrument to propose marriage, which is why he was so keen to give it to Zaharah personally.
It was not, at this time, a proposal, but when Anthony and Zaharah did get married, five years later, there was an unusual guest, standing at the back. A tall man in a dark suit with chubby cheeks.

NVDA – Nonviolent Direct Action

> *"Darkness cannot drive out darkness: only light can do that. Hate cannot drive out hate: only love can do that. The beauty of nonviolence is that in its own way and in its own time it seeks to break the chain reaction of evil'.'*
> – Martin Luther King

History

Nonviolence or *Ahimsa* can be traced back to ancient Hindu scholars and extensively explored in Janism. The principle that any violence has Karmic consequences sits alongside the belief that as we all have a divine spark connecting us, any harm done to others is done to ourselves.

Christians could say that Jesus was advocating nonviolent resistance when he said during the Sermon on the Mount, "That ye resist not evil: but whosoever shall smite thee on thy right cheek, turn to him the other also."

Mohandas Gandhi (1869 – 1948) an Indian lawyer, employed nonviolent resistance to lead the successful campaign for India's independence.

He wrote that British rule was established in India with the co-operation of Indians and had survived only because of this cooperation. If Indians refused to cooperate, British rule would collapse. In 1930, he led a Satyagraha (truth-insistence) march against the British salt tax laws and was arrested for making salt. This inspired large scale acts of civil disobedience leading to the jailing of over 60,000 Indians.

"The essence of nonviolent technique is that it seeks to liquidate antagonisms but not the antagonists." – Ghandi

In the mid 17th century, the Quaker Peace Testimony, deriving from the belief that God is in everyone, turned a refusal to bear arms into a way of life and in 1934, Quaker lawyer Richard Gregg described nonviolence as moral jiu-jitsu – the opponent expects resistance and when there is none, he loses his moral balance.

Nonviolence is distinct from a passive acceptance of superior force. It implies:
- a willingness to take action without giving in to or resorting to violence
- a respect for everyone involved in a conflict
- a refusal to do harm to people or living things, and
- a willingness to take suffering on oneself without inflicting it on others.

Quakersintheworld.org

Two of the founders of Greenpeace, Irving and Dorothy Stowe, were Quakers and they instilled the principles of nonviolence and bearing witness into the organisation, which remains, to this day, at its heart.

All Greenpeace activists are trained in nonviolent direct action to ensure they understand the principles, the practice, reasons why it is used and to weed out anyone who may not be relied upon to maintain these principles.

Why?
Because it works.

Nonviolent strategies have consistently proved to be an effective way of creating lasting change within society.

When violence is used, someone usually ends up hurt, resentful and looking for revenge. The struggle can last generations. While a peaceful resolution can leave the society working together for the benefit of all.

It isn't always the case, there have been any number of bloody revolutions throughout history, but research covering the 20th Century, shows that a non-violent struggle is more likely to succeed.[2]

A demonstration that descends into violent conflict can be more easily dismissed and crushed by authority while the message is diluted and lost. To this end, it's been known that agent provocateurs have been embedded in protests.

Violence often has its roots in fear. Greenpeace always ensure their actions are peaceful, there's a clue in the name, and police know what to expect, they know it is not going to 'kick off.' Occasionally violence has been inflicted upon activists (see Brussels), but the response has always been peaceful. It maintains the moral high ground and engenders public support.

This is why we use nonviolent direct action.

---

2. Erica Chenoweth: *Why Civil Resistance Works.*

Breaking the Law

"Civil disobedience on grounds of conscience is an honourable tradition in this country and those who take part in it may in the end be vindicated by history."
– Lord Justice Hoffman

A law is usually something that cannot be broken, such as the laws of physics or nature. Common law is derived through time-tested customs and precedents. Statutes are rules imposed by governments to regulate society. Usually these rules are there for good reasons, occasionally, they are not, but that's a different story.

When environmental activists break the law, it's because they know that all the lawful activities they've done up to that point have not been enough. They do it to bring attention to an issue, to shine a spotlight on a wrongdoing and to try to prevent a far greater crime happening.

Climate change/heating is destroying lives now. Nature is collapsing around us and it's the quest for profit that's driving it. Our greenhouse gas emissions have already pushed the planet past tipping points on the roller-coaster of chaos towards a hot-house Earth where all life will struggle to survive. We are talking mass genocide and ecocide. The actions of activists simply do not compare at this scale. Our governments, the people we elect to keep us safe and regulate our societies, have allowed this to happen, they have broken the social contract between the governing and the governed. If their laws are broken, it's because physics and nature have laws that cannot be broken.

Virtuti non armis fido
(I trust to virtue not to arms)

The Kidlington Airport Debacle

The tail end of November is hanging onto the last warmth of autumn as Marty and I walk around the outskirts of Oxford city. I had agreed to meet him after learning that Thames Valley Climate Action needed a van to transport some equipment to an action. I have a white escort van and so long as it's just driving stuff about, I'm happy to help.

Marty is tall and young, a flop of dark brown hair attempting to cover one eye.

'I've bought some crowd control barriers,' he says, 'and I need help picking them up this afternoon if possible and then, on the morning, delivering them to a spot off the A44, along with some other bits and bobs.'

'Yeah, I think I can manage that.'

'It will be an early start, 5am. The target is Kidlington Airport.'

'Ah, the recently re-branded Oxford International.'

'The first scheduled flight is due on Saturday morning and we'll be there to meet it. You know that aviation emissions at altitude is a much bigger problem than the industry is making out?'

'I do, yes,' I reply.

'And that up and down the country, airports are trying to expand even though we're meant to be reducing our emissions?'

'It's crazy. They only care about "growing the business".'

'Well, we'll be growing something else – guerrilla gardening.'

Guerrilla gardening is the subversive activity of planting vegetables or flowers in an often, but not necessarily, Council owned, unused area.

'Could that be classed as criminal damage?' I ask.

Marty screws his face up. 'Possibly, the main thing is to get onto the runway with the barriers.'

I fetch my van and we drive out to a yard where the crowd control barriers are stored. Loading up, they are a little too long so I tie the rear doors together and dropping Marty off, I return home to the small barn conversion Janet and I are renting in Nuneham Courtney, a village south of the city. The barn is set in a courtyard with other outbuildings and the farmhouse where our landlord and his wife live. It's a lovely rural location that we can just about afford with Janet working at a nearby environmental charity and me working in a bike shop in Abingdon.

The barriers have been sitting in my van, in the courtyard outside, for a couple of days, not going anywhere. It's dark, sometime in the middle of the night, I am in bed, not sleeping well as I know I have to get up around 4am but slipping in and out of slumber. Something brings my mind to the surface, a noise outside, a memory of a noise that sounded like a car door closing gently. I'm dreaming it, surely, no one would be outside in the courtyard, but all the same I force myself awake, listening intently. Nothing, silence, time and sleep take over.

My alarm brings me to the surface again. 4am. I get up and get dressed in my work clothes. I need to be in Abingdon for the bike shop opening at eight, so I should have time to nip home after the delivery to make sandwiches.

I drive into the city, down an older residential street in Jericho, to a house where the participants of the action are meeting.

Inside, Marty is making breakfast, falafels I think but I'm not sure, the smell of frying drifts from the kitchen. His girlfriend, Jenny appears dressed in full tweed including flat cap, her long wavy hair tucked underneath.

She notices my bleary-eyed surprise. 'It's the whole gardening look,' she says.

I mouth an 'Oh.'

Also there, sitting on the sofa, is Stuart, dressed more casually in blue jeans, his long hair drapes around his shoulders. Another man and woman, both fair, young and attractive, looking like a couple, are introduced as Tony and Samantha.

The room is tense with pre-action nerves, fidgeting with clothes and details. Coffee being gulped, breakfast stuck in tightened throats. Jenny uses the bathroom for the second time in the half hour I've been there. They're waiting on a taxi.

'A taxi to an action?' I ask.

'We don't drive.'

They load gardening tools into the back of the van as the taxi arrives and the house empties. Stuart is coming with me. We leave a couple of minutes after them to avoid raising the taxi driver's suspicions.

We wind our way through the streets of Oxford. Still dark and quiet. Meeting only the occasional early morning delivery van. Through Summertown and out onto the A44. I check the mirror as we come off a roundabout, a set of headlights a fair way back, nothing to worry about.

We pass a side road as we lose the street lights for open countryside.

'How much further?' I ask Stuart. We are now on a dual carriageway.

'A little way yet, there should be a pull in.' He leans forward, looking for landmarks in the dark. In the distance there are red lights.

Then three things happen at once. Stuart's phone rings, it's Marty. 'Abort!'

The lights ahead turn blue. Suddenly a police car is beside us and another behind, we are surrounded by flashing lights. I coast to a stop. In front of us is the taxi, already pulled over by the police. The car alongside stops, blocking the lane and an officer gets out, comes towards us.

'What do I say?' I ask Stuart. He shrugs, his face is pale.

I wind the window down. The police officer is older than I expect, fifties maybe? Grey hair poking from under the cap. He squats beside my door.

'Is this your vehicle?' he asks.

'Yes.'

'Where are you going?'

'To work.'

'What kind of work is that?'

I hesitate, my mind desperately juggling different questions. Should I lie to him? Can I actually think of a lie? Is there really any point? Answers come quickly, no, no and no. I look at him blankly.

'Right, I'm arresting you on suspicion of going equipped to commit criminal damage. You do not have to say anything, but it may harm your defence if you do not mention when questioned something which you later rely on in court. Anything you do say may be given in evidence. Step out of the vehicle.'

I am escorted to a police car and as I look up the road I can see the four from the taxi being fed into a van.

We are driven to Abingdon Police Station and gathered together in the holding cell. The processing seems to take ages. Jenny asks to use a toilet but is denied, repeatedly being told to sit down. She curls up the wooden slat seat, obviously in pain.

At last, I am deposited in a cell. High on one wall is a window of thick glass blocks which lighten as dawn breaks. Right now, I should be making sandwiches for work. I wasn't expecting this and it screws with my head. I try to sleep but have stress hormones aching in my chest. When will I be let out of here?

Time passes with a mini break of microwave chips and baked beans in a small polystyrene tray and a cup of tea, also in polystyrene.

At some point, my solicitor arrives and we are treated to a police interview to which I answer 'No comment' to questions.

Back in the cell, as I pace the small space, I watch the sunlight through the glass blocks start to diminish, eventually going dark.

'For pity sake, how much longer?' I demand of the steel door. I want to go home, I never signed up for this, just drop the guys off and get on with my day, but that's not happening.

Finally an officer comes for me. My possessions are returned but not my phone. A piece of paper with bail conditions is presented for me to sign. I am not allowed outside my home address between midnight and 6am. I can stay at another address but must notify a CID officer named Biddle, while the officer granting bail is called Fiddler. I'm hoping that when they retire, these two will get together to start a law firm.

'When can I get my van?' I ask the Desk Sergeant.

'It's evidence.'

'I need it for work.'

He takes a deep breath and holds it for a moment before exhaling loudly. 'Pick it up next week.'

I am released into the evening gloom. I look around for any support from the activist group but there is none. It's getting chilly as I walk to the bus stop. I didn't bring a coat as I expected to be in the comfort of a warm vehicle.

I find a bus towards Oxford. I get off at Redbridge and wait for a bus that will take me to Nuneham. It's getting late and I'm so tired. My vision is blurred and the orange lights of the bus numbers become a dancing smudge. Because of this, I miss the last one of the night. So I start walking the four miles home.

As I reach the gate, I can see Janet's car is out. I don't have my door keys so stand in the courtyard, shivering, it's past midnight and proper winter cold. My landlord, Richard, has keys but their house lights are off. I wait but my head is thumping, my body aches. I yearn to be warm. I walk over to their house and knock. A few minutes later, Richard's wife opens the door in her dressing gown, frowning, serious, not pleased to see me.

'I haven't got my keys.'

Her face softens when she sees the state I'm in.

'I was going to throw these at you,' she says handing me the spare set. 'We've had the police here, going through all our barns.'

I groan and close my eyes.

'I'm so sorry, it wasn't... I never meant...'

'Get yourself inside, I think Janet is out looking for you.'

I groan again and turn back to our own door.

Footnote:
Janet returned a little later and gave me a right tongue-lashing then a big hug. It transpired that the police had thoroughly searched our home, confiscating Janet's work laptop and anything else they could argue might incriminate me.
We were on bail and under the curfew, for eight months before the case was dropped. Thames Valley Climate Action had arranged for police station support but they had gone for chips when the Police chose to release me.
It seems like the tip-off had come from an undercover cop who had infiltrated the group.

Shell Garages

It's already light, dawn comes early in mid July but grey clouds fill the sky. Teams are finding their pre-booked Zip (short-hire) cars, spread out across Greater London. We've been told that we must not start before 5am.

In the media hub, campaigners clutching mugs of steaming coffee, wait for images and video. Hushed discussions as the studio is readied for a day's broadcasting on the Greenpeace channel. It's a new angle they are trying, hoping people will tune in to follow the action.

When we were first asked to lead teams for this action, about a month ago, Janet and I both realised we would be in for a stressful time. Even the intervening weeks have been filled with tense discussions in our living room on repercussions and nervous studying of road maps.

It's part of a long campaign. Royal Dutch Shell are planning to drill for oil in the fragile Arctic environment and Greenpeace are searching for ways to prevent them. Pressure is building and public opinion is starting to be noticed by the politicians who issue licences. The company must be concerned about the damage we are causing their brand.

Today we are going to try to shut down every Shell garage within the M25 motorway that rings the capital, and several in Edinburgh, 100 in total.

Roughly twenty teams of four, each with five petrol stations on their hit list are making their way to their first targets. Some in hire cars, some on push bikes. We think the first ones will be fairly easy but it will get tougher as the day progresses and word gets around.

We are in our Zip car, an automatic which I'm not used to driving and almost put Tony through the windscreen at the first junction by incorrectly using my left foot. Tony is navigating off a smart phone next to me. In the back are Gail and Lyn from the Preston group. Leaving Croydon for leafy suburbs, we spot a big Shell logo dominating the display tower on the corner of a small junction. The forecourt is almost empty, perfect. Turning right we find a side street and park up. We get out and fetch the equipment from the boot. Each knows their role, each has a job to do. Hearts are beating hard and Gail turns to walk back to the garage.

'Wait,' I say. 'Let's just pause a moment, think about what we are going to do.' My fingers are trembling as I check the tools, a screwdriver, pliers and short stepladder. The others are looking at me expectantly.

'Ready?'

They nod.

'Okay, let's do this.'

At the same time, Janet's team are walking onto a forecourt near Harrow. Her job is to enter the shop and speak to the staff. She's carrying a letter and a notice giving directions to the nearest alternative petrol station which she sticks to the door as she walks in. There is a woman paying at the till so Janet looks out of the window watching her team at work, as she waits in line. The woman ahead walks past her and Janet takes a deep breath as she steps up to the counter. On the other side, the young man is staring with a half open mouth at the scene outside. He has a dark, Asian appearance, smartly dressed in a red, corporate polo shirt.

'We're an Emergency Response Team,' Janet says. 'Don't worry, don't panic. We are shutting the fuel off for the sake of Arctic safety. What you need to do is give this letter to your manager, it makes it clear why we are doing this.'

The young man's mouth drops full open as he takes the letter, he's trying to think of something to say but cannot. Janet turns on her heel and leaves the shop with a fast walk.

My team are now walking onto our station's forecourt. Tony has an Iphone clipped to his hi-viz jacket and he talks into it.

'This is team Arctic Fox going into Hensley Wood Shell station.' There is a stack of traffic cones which he quickly puts across the entrance. Lyn is walking into the shop as I place the stepladder against the outside wall. Tony joins Gail who is removing the pump nozzles and securing them together with a bike lock. A customer is already filling up.

'Sorry about this,' Tony says to him. 'The fuel is going to stop in one minute, if you could pay for what you've got, an alternative station is being pasted on the door.'

The man looks confused but submits to the authority of the hi-viz jacket.

On every petrol station forecourt, you will find a little red box with an emergency stop switch. This cuts the power to all the pumps in case of a spill or accident. They are usually mounted outside the shop, at arm's reach and I am standing on a stepladder to work on it. I have switched the power off and now removing screws holding the cover on. Inside there is a contact bar which I take out using pliers. Then unscrewing the switch handle, I put both in my pocket before replacing the cover. The attendant indoors is banging on the window and shouting for me to stop what I'm doing. Lyn emerges from the shop as I pick up the steps and call to the others.

'We're done, let's go.'

We all start to walk away but then break into a jog as we reach the pavement. Rounding the corner to the car, I notice a post box.

'Lyn, do you have an envelope?'

'Yeah, got them here.' She fishes inside her coat and produces a brown manila stamped envelope with the address of Shell's CEO ready printed on the front, inside is a letter to him.

I put the switch handle and contact bar into the envelope and post it.

Theft is defined as the intention to permanently deprive someone of something. We're not stealing them, we're sending them back.

We jump into the car and drive onto to the next filling station on the list.

Janet's team have completed their third Shell station and decided they need a cup of tea.

'There's a café.' Jane points ahead to the other side of the road. Janet pulls over. 'Right,' she says. 'Remember not to talk about this in there, we don't know who's listening. How's everyone feeling?'

'I'm a bag of nerves,' Emma says from the back.

'Me too,' John says. 'It's like when I had to give a best man's speech, times ten.'

'I'm finding it hard,' Janet says. 'It's not so bad for the customers, they can go fill up somewhere else. It's the guys in the shop I feel for, they're just trying to make a living. I have to say I'm conflicted.'

The tea is a welcome distraction of normality amidst the crazy morning but the break makes resuming the enterprise worse.

We are now in our second zip car having swapped back in Croydon in case the number plates had been clocked. It's late morning and we've shut down three garages. We drive past the fourth and there is a police car sitting on the forecourt, so we keep going. Word is certainly out now and it's starting to feel like a game of cat and mouse.

'Onto the next one?' I suggest.

'How far is it?' Lyn asks.

Tony checks the phone screen. 'About five miles. Anyone else hungry?'

'I could do with a cup of tea,' Lyn says.

'I'm not sure I could eat anything, stomach's a complete knot,' I say, 'but it would be good to take a break. Let's find a café somewhere quiet.'

Janet's team have just completed their fourth service station and are walking away when a car comes swinging off the forecourt behind them.

The driver shouts, 'I'M CALLING THE POLICE. I KNOW WHAT YOU'VE DONE, I'M CALLING THE POLICE.'

They hurry down the road with the car following them. Janet is carrying a big bag of bike locks but as they get to their Zip car, the driver following parks across it, blocking them in.

'Okay,' Janet says. 'We'll go on foot.' They carry on and turn up a side-street but the driver is still tracking them. It's a cul-de-sac and soon they are back on the main road.

'What do we do now?'

Janet looks over her shoulder and can see the car waiting to pull out. Just beyond the corner and almost out of view is a large bush beside a brown panel fence. 'Let's hide behind that.' She points at it.

My team are back on the road and we're taking another look at Coulsdon road garage. The police car is still there.

'I can't believe the coppers are just waiting there.'

'There's no one in the car,' Tony says.

'Do you think they've just left the car there as a deterrent?' Gail says.

'Shall we do it anyway?' Lyn says.

I turn down a side-road and park. 'What do we think, unnecessary risk?'

Behind me, Gail's face is blank, she doesn't really care, but Lyn is nodding.

'I think you're right,' Tony says. 'Unnecessary risk, we've another two on the list.'

I put the car into gear. 'Okay, next one then?'

Tony reads out the address and swipes the screen of the phone.

I've driven these roads a few times now and starting to recognise landmarks. The next filling station appears on the left. Lyn has the location of the nearest alternative ready written out, all we need to do is find somewhere to park.

I spot a side-road but it's double yellows – no parking. I turn in anyway and a second left takes us into a residential area with parking. It's a bit of a walk but probably the closest we'll find.

Tony gets a call from the media team, they want us to film this one as people are tuning in to watch us live, so he turns on the Iphone camera as we walk onto the forecourt. It's clear the staff have been made aware of our activities so we need to be fast and the team is now well practised but the screws on the emergency stop switch are rusty and I'm struggling to free them.

Lyn is standing behind the ladder. 'C'mon, we're all done. We need to go.'

Tony is also waiting for me, I glance over at him, he's still filming. *I'm going to have to do this*, I think. 'Just give me a minute, I want this one.'

It's always the last screw that's worst, most rusted and reluctant to move. Putting all my weight against it, the screwdriver grips the head and the tiniest of movement means it's free. I quickly undo it and get the cover off, removing the contact bar, but the screw holding the switch handle is too far gone.

'C'mon Pete, the manager's coming out now,' Lyn says.

The power is off and with the bar out cannot be turned back on, so I pop the cover back and jump down the ladder. 'Okay, let's go.'

Gail is already halfway to the road.

As we scoot back to the car, I keep looking over my shoulder expecting the manager to be chasing but I see no one. Calmly driving away out of the residential area and onto a main road, I explode with a series of profanities, a release of tension that has become unbearable. I glance in the rear view mirror at the surprised faces of the older women in the back. 'Sorry,' I say. Lyn is smiling but Gail's expression is still blank.

Janet parts the branches to peer out. 'He's still sitting there waiting.'

'Can he see us in here?'

'Probably, we must look right idiots, hiding in a bush.'

'Anyone with a better idea?'

'There's a bus coming.'

'So?'

'There's a bus stop, right there, we just jump on it.'

'What about the Zip car?'

'Sod the car, we'll tell them where to find it.'

'Good plan, let's go.'

The bus stops and they run from behind the bush to get on.

'Where to?' the driver asks.

'Errm, a café?'

'A café?' the driver screws up his face.

'The train station.'

'Which is it to be, café or train station,' he huffs.

'Train station.'

A woman sitting in a front seat pipes up, 'It's the other side of the road for the train station. You want to be going the other way.'

'Just, ahhh, just take us to the town centre and we'll work it out from there.'

The driver smirks. 'Watford is three pound ten each.'

Janet hands him a twenty and bobs up and down as he counts out the change, the others find seats.

With the coins in her pocket, Janet turns to face the rest of the passengers who are watching curiously. Through the rear window she can see the flashing lights of a police car. She grabs a bar as the driver starts to pull away. A siren wails and the blood drains from her face as she drops the bag of bike locks and swings down onto a seat. The flashing lights overtake and slew to a halt in front of the bus. The driver jumps on the brakes and the vehicle jolts to a stop. Janet tries to swallow but her mouth is too dry, she glances across at Emma whose wide eyes are staring ahead.

Two male police officers board the bus. 'We're looking for some people who may have committed a crime.'

Janet can feel the eyes of the passengers boring into the back of her head.

An officer takes a step forward, he's almost alongside Janet and Emma. 'No one is going anywhere until we find–'

Janet stands up. 'I think you're looking for us.'

The next garage is proving to be a problem for us. There is simply nowhere handy to park. The only space we can find is down a one way residential street with cars parked on both sides. As we open the boot to get the gear out, Tony looks up the road. The petrol station is at the far end, across a junction.

'I don't like it,' he says.

I follow his gaze, if anything goes wrong, we will have to drive up a tight one-way street, almost past the garage, to get away.

'Shall we call it a day?' I ask the team.

Gail shrugs, 'I don't mind.'

Lyn and Tony are nodding. We've had almost ten hours of tension with heart bursting surges of adrenaline. We were emotionally drained and this did not bode well.

'Okay, let's go home.'

After returning the Zip car to its allotted parking place, I take the remaining equipment back to the Greenpeace warehouse. I am the last one in and welcomed with a cheer. Patrick slaps my back.

'Well done for getting back. We've shut down 74.'

'Not everyone made it?'

'No, there have been some arrests.'

I look around the crowd of faces. Janet is missing. My body sags. It's been a long day and the repetitive bouts of anxiety have taken their toll. I make a cup of tea and find a sofa in a quiet corner to collapse on.

Emily comes over. 'You okay?'

'Yeah, knackered. Don't think I'm going to be catching the last train back to Wales.'

'No worries, we'll sort a bed for you tonight. A few are staying over.'

The next morning we are in a café in Islington, waiting for the arrestees who have just been released after being held overnight. Summer sunlight and the smell of frying bacon fills the interior.

Janet and Emma walk in both wearing police issue, paper trousers barely concealing the colour of their knickers underneath.

I give Janet a big hug.

'They took my best jeans,' she exclaims.

'Why?'

'Evidence apparently.'

'Evidence? What... how?'

Janet shakes her head then looks over at the counter. 'Dying for a cuppa.'

'You get some breakfast and I'll run down to the charity shop for jeans. What size are you?'

'No, I'll come. Goodness knows what you'll come back with.' She smiles and grabs my arm.

A Climbing Action

Upstairs in the warehouse, one end has been laid out with a kitchen and lounge area. Light twists its way in through tall windows with protest banners acting as curtains. Wiola joins Daniel and Sandra on the sofas surrounding a long coffee table covered in printouts and drawings.

Sandra is mid-twenties, this will be her first big climbing action for Greenpeace. Her long black hair flows over her shoulder as she looks away. 'I'm sorry, I don't know what happened. I wake up and it really hurts.'

'Is it your back?' Wiola asks.

Sandra nods, still staring into the corner of the room.

Dan looks between the women. 'Can we bring in someone to replace you?

'No, no,' Wiola protests. 'Not now, we have been working together for so long, it would feel wrong and anyway, no one else knows about this, how could we bring them in with just a day to go?'

Dan nods. 'Yeah, you're right, unless I do it?'

Dan has been helping the women with the organisation and their training.

'This is possible.' Sandra's head drops a little further.

'You are the only one who could,' Wiola says.

'Well, let's see what your back is like in the morning,' Dan says. 'I'll get my kit and be ready to step in. Only problem is...' Dan leans forward, 'I'm already on police bail.'

It is still dark, very early morning, figures move silently between the warehouse and the vehicle. The occasional clink of carabiners as the climbers get into the back of a Luton van, followed by the support team.

Someone whispers, 'Good luck.' Gates are opened and the van drives out. In the back, twelve people sit in complete darkness, listening to the road noise and sensing the vehicle's movements. Six young women, in climbing harnesses and helmets on makeshift seats are at the front of the space, crowded around a triple extension ladder. Filling the back of the van are the all male support crew, of which I am one.

While Shell prepared to drill for oil in the harsh environment of the Arctic, where any leaks would be a disaster for the fragile ecosystems, the climb team had been practising hanging off buildings, climbing towers and making plans with models. Drawn from an international pool, they now look calm, never betraying the fear just below the surface. Fear that they might fail, let the team down and fear of something none of them could anticipate – what it will feel like to be hanging off the side of a building that high. What they are about to do is safe only if they all remember their training and make no mistakes, but there were unknown elements that could literally throw it all into the air.

The support team, recruited with an obscure message about being "good with heights," have only trained for a couple of days. We have to open a hatch that's been cut in the roof of the van, extend the ladders, then haul a platform and kit bags onto a building. Then it's over to the women.

The drive seems to take ages. Nervous glances are exchanged at every stop, until the vehicle moves off again, and then a brief call on the two-way radio, 'Get ready.'

The van slows, there's a bump as it mounts a kerb then stops.

The radio again, 'Go, go, go.'

Andy is already undoing the catch for the roof and pushes the hatch out of the way. The dim blue of early morning light streams inside. Mark, six foot two with tree-trunk legs poking out from shorts, is pushing the heavy ladders up through the gap and against a strange metal building, at least three stories high, that turns out to be the housing of a massive air-conditioning unit for London Bridge Train Station.

With the top of the ladder resting precariously against a bank of metal fins, Mark starts to climb, I pass him the platform and follow him up the ladder. With the necessity of speed, the usual safety policy of only one person at a time is ignored and the support team and the climbers are soon all standing on the metal building. Andy is in charge and carries the platform. This will be the bridge to cross over the gap onto the next building.

As rehearsed many times the previous day, Andy and I carefully position the platform upright on the edge of the flat roof. The building opposite is the entrance to the underground station, its glass roof is about nine feet away. Jeff, Ben and Mark grab the rope leading to the other end of the platform and slowly lower. The climbers watch, eager to get started. The platform drops but misses the adjacent roof. It's too short. A muffled cry of 'What?' comes from one of the women, months of preparation to be foiled by a stupid miscalculation?

It's difficult to pull the scaffold platform up once it had gone past its centre of balance, but Mark heaves on the rope and up it comes.

Below a security guard calls up, 'Hey, what are you doing?'

'Stand back,' I shout down to him.

'Pete, focus!' Andy orders. 'In the gutter.' He nods at the steel channel running just below the lip of the roof.

Together we drop it into the gutter.

'Okay, lower again,' Andy says and the others let the top of the platform down. This time it reaches with about two inches resting on the other side.

'Is it safe?' I ask, looking at the flimsy guttering but Andy is already striding across the bridge. He makes it over. *Oh well*, I think, *may as well get it over with*. I step onto the platform, carefully placing one foot in front of the other. The bridge is about 18 inches wide and the thirty foot drop is enough to make my heart race. I focus on Andy waiting for me on the other side. When I reach the glass roof on the other side, my relief is tainted by seeing figures walking beneath me. The rest follow including the climbers. Everyone watches as Mark, the biggest of them all, makes his way over the platform. When he reaches the glass roof, he sighs then looks down.

'Oh my...'

'Stick to the beams, Mark,' Ben warns.

'It should be fine.' Andy is already heading off towards the base of the target building.

'That's easy for you to say,' Mark mutters, following on behind.

On the roof of the railway station, they split into two teams, each one there to help get the climbers started. Dan has his climbing harness and is following Sandra.

'This is it, Sandra, how do you feel, how's your back?'

'It's okay.' She is nodding vigorously.

'Are you sure, last chance?'

'I can do this.'

They both look up at the immense building towering above them. The sun is rising over the London skyline and lights up the glass in ice-like refractions. At 300m The Shard is the tallest building in Western Europe.

Dan looks into her eyes. Resolution. 'Good luck,' he says and jogs back across the glass roof as police sirens wail their arrival. He runs back over the bridge and scoots down the ladder, jumping off at the van roof, sliding over the windscreen, snapping a wiper blade and landing on the ground beside. He walks away swiftly, as if he had nothing at all to do with anything.

Getting the initial lines attached is taking far too long. The women have a long, hard climb ahead and need to get going. Frustration is mounting. The radio Andy is carrying breaks into life. 'What's taking so long? Over,' says the Action Co-ordinator on the ground.

'Yeah, we've had some difficulty hooking over the first bar but they're on now and starting to climb. Over,' Andy replies.

'Okay, great. Let me know if there are any other problems. Out.'

With the women away and climbing, the support crew convene to discuss their exit strategy. There may be an option of escaping through a building site on the other side of the station. Andy radios the AC for advice. A few moments later the AC replies saying that the station is due to open in ten minutes and the Transport Police are keen to get them off the roof so if they come down now, they won't be arrested.

Without the adrenaline and in full daylight, walking back over the bridge is a little more challenging. I take a deep breath before embarking, Jeff decides to do it on all fours while Ben, perversely, runs over it. Down the ladder we go and into the back of the van. Discarding hard hats and hi-viz, we emerge and quickly leave the scene for a café breakfast.

The climbers are not having an easy time. Being weighed down with bags and a huge banner, everything is taking longer than expected. By midday they are barely halfway.

The media have picked up on the story and are loving it. Londoners are grabbing their binoculars and following the climbers during their lunch breaks.

I get a phone call from Janet. 'It's wonderful!' she says.'Such a good action.'

'Is it?' I hadn't realised how big it had become.

'Yes.' There is a pause. 'I'm almost in tears.'

Sandra is now in a lot of pain from her back and has had to swap places with Wiola taking the lead. Halfway up the Shard and Wiola needs to pee and is trying to get the security and police, who are watching her progress from inside the building, to turn around. She has a 'She-Wee' system that sometimes works.

Ali is below her, waving through the glass to a corporate meeting. She gets a shower from above.

As evening approaches, the wind is picking up and it's becoming clear that the banner of a polar bear, big enough to be seen by the oil executives in the Shell building across the river, would be too dangerous to deploy. The climbers are very tired but nearing the top.

They have been climbing for over fourteen hours and with just fifty metres left, they have a radio conference. It's decided they cannot go any further, but Wiola has reserves of strength and wants to keep going. They agree that she can carry on alone to try to reach the top. Incredibly, at a quarter of a kilometre off the ground, she starts to free climb the last section. It is different to the rest of the structure, more complicated and one large beam is causing her a problem. People are watching from the top floor, including police and security. Three times she tries to get around the beam and with each failure there is a groan from the small crowd. The fourth attempt and she makes it. On the other side, she stops for a moment to get her breath, her muscles are aching like hell so she focuses on the view, looking over the city and this clear summer's day. She is aware this is a life-moment and drinks in the energy from the air itself. Love for the natural world is why she is here, it's what got her here and it will get her to the top. She starts to climb again.

With just a few metres to go, Wiola is confronted by police climbers on the opposite side of a pillar. She spots the ropes they rigged to the top.

'Are these your ropes?' she asks.

A young man replies in Polish, 'Yes, they are for your safety.'

'Ah, you are Polish too? Can you check them for me?'

He goes off to check and returns. 'Yes, they are safe, you can use them.'

Wiola transfers to their ropes and makes it to the top platform.

Cheers break out, not just in the offices and on the streets of London, but across the country as viewers on social media and the news watch her unfurl a small but clearly visible banner saying, "SAVE THE ARCTIC."

The Gift of Solar

It's Christmas 2015 and the then Chancellor, George Osborne, had recently cut subsidies to home solar power generation. So a small organisation called 10:10 Climate Action, ran a campaign called *Keep FITS*, referring to the feed in tariffs. As it was the season of goodwill, they decided to send George a gift.

Ant is a director of a renewable energy firm, so we were given the task of installing solar panels on his constituency office roof.

This is a posh area of Cheshire called Tatton and George's office is in a grand old building which is surprisingly tall.

We arrive in the pre-dawn darkness. Pulling into the car park, we don our fluorescent green coats and hard hats. Ant has loaded scaffolding to access the roof in a trailer and solar panels in the back of the van. Wasting no time, we set up the scaffolding behind the commercial sized wheelie bins. All is going well except the tower is too short and a ladder has to be improvised on top, much to the derision of passing builders.

'Oi, you're not allowed to do that,' they shout.

I know, thinks Ant.

We are joined by a small media crew and the comedian Josie Long to film the escapade.

As the sun rises, the scaffolding is complete and we stack the solar panels against the wall, ready to be lifted onto the roof. Ant climbs the tower to rig up a rope hoist system.

Josie does a piece to camera explaining how solar energy has added £3.3 billion to the economy along with 35,000 jobs but George's cuts are threatening the whole industry.

At this point some interference arrives in the shape of a short robust man and a tall stroppy fella in tweed. Even his flat cap reeks of conservative so we guess he might be an acquaintance of Mr Osborne's and Josie attempts to explain the gift we were giving while Ant and me resolutely ignore him.

Mr Tweed strides backwards and forwards insisting we stop and getting frustrated that nobody is listening to him.

'Look, I told you not to do that,' he says as I send another panel skywards.

'Oh dear,' Josie says, biting her knuckles.

I can't think of anything to say to get rid of the guy so I point to his head saying, 'You should have a hard hat on, mate.'

He turns his attention to the cameraman.

'If you film me on this property one more time, I'll drag you down the street.'

The short round man is on his phone and it isn't long before a police officer arrives. The game is up and we can do no more. Ant climbs down in time to stop the film producer from winding up the constable.

Names are taken as we sadly load the panels back into the van and go in search of a café for breakfast.

Josie is on the phone, 'Hi, is that Boris Johnson's office? We were wondering if he would like a gift of solar panels...'

Brussels

An interview with Jeff Rice.

I first met Jeff on the Houses of Parliament action. Originally from Nottingham, he has long dark hair, now starting to grey, usually tied in a pony-tail, and goatie beard. He's been involved with Greenpeace for many years. With his easygoing humour and conversational nature, everyone who meets Jeff ends up being a friend, except for anti-wind farm campaigners, for whom he is a scourge. We held this interview over the internet during the Coronavirus lockdown.

PB: 'Jeff, I was thinking about the time I had a brush with the Belgium Police and remembered you getting beaten up by them, would you like to tell the tale?'

JR: 'It was a very big action, with over 300 people taking part. When you have that many, from all over the EU, it really feels like a large section of the planet, all pulling together. Our teams were constructed in such a way as to mix up the nationalities and presumably build that feeling of the event being an international effort.'

PB: 'Where were you and why?'

JR: 'In Brussels, the European Council building. Inside, finance ministers from 27 nations were failing to commit necessary funding to reduce carbon emissions. We were there to say, "You're not leaving until you do."

'The city was quiet as we closed in on our target, walking in small groups, in the cool morning air. I love this moment; the quiet immediately before an action. You realise the police haven't got wind of what you're about to do and you'll probably be able to pull it off.'

PB: 'Were you nervous?'

JR: 'Not really. You always get that weird feeling in your gut, but I've been doing actions for years so it was more excitement than nerves. I was walking with a young activist from the UK, it was her first action and she was anxious. Sometimes just talking about it can help, so we chatted as we walked.

'And so, we arrived and quite simply sat and blocked the entrance to the EU headquarters. Our message was very simple; finance ministers should devote billions of Euros to help poor nations tackle climate change. "Save the climate, bail out the planet." This was just after the banks had been saved from the 2008 crash, so perfectly reasonable, you might think; certainly in these more enlightened times. If you can do it for banks, why not the climate?

'We sat and blocked and waited. The stone floor was cold to sit on, fortunately this had been anticipated and we all brought cardboard or foam. It's important on these things to be prepared for boredom. It's like some bizarre form of meditation.

'After an hour or so, the police, having just been monitoring us up until this point, began to act. The mood changes and you get a slight sense of foreboding, *what are they up to?* First, they moved spectators away, beyond being able to see us. I think most of us found that rather ominous. I started to worry at that point. It was like the police didn't want the public or media to see what they were about to do. Then they started to remove the protestors, one by one. Any that put up the slightest resistance were met with violence. This seemed to vary on... well, I'm not entirely sure. Did the cops just not like the look of some people? There were quite a few cries of pain as people were removed and you can't help but feel for your friends and colleagues as you sit there watching them have a difficult time at the hands of the cops. *Aren't the police supposed to be a force for good?* you ask yourself. It makes you wonder just who it is they are protecting. We were there in peaceful protest, to get EU leaders to act on climate change.

'I saw one of my UK friends put up zero resistance. This was entirely reasonable and saved him from harm, but I couldn't resist winding him up later for his "feeble efforts." I decided, when the time came, to offer a low level of resistance and give up the instant that it became painful. An officer approached me and began "feeling me" for some hold points. Rather disconcerting. He finally settled on my head, gripping the hood of my jacket, plus hat underneath. He pulled so hard, the hood ripped off. I never did see that hat again. Undeterred, he went for my head again, this time grasping a fistful of hair. And he pulled.

PB: 'Ouch, that must have hurt.'

JR: 'This was when the onslaught of pain started for me and events became something of a blur. I felt like I was being pulled in multiple directions. I didn't know what my body was doing. I just felt universal pain.

'My plan of offering minimal resistance had failed instantly. Unfortunately, the activist behind me decided that he was going to help by wrapping his legs around my waist to stop me being pulled away. Note to activists – NEVER let this happen to you. Even though some other guy was resisting on my behalf, the cops chose to beat ME up. Oh, if only they'd have beaten him up! I did feel a little angry towards this other activist – someone I'd never even met before. Later he apologised and said he didn't realise what they would do to me. I gritted my teeth and reassured him that everything was "fine."

'What happened next, as I say, was a blur. I remember cops kneeling on my head, kneeling on my back, punching me repeatedly in the face, pulling out chunks of hair and eventually getting my hands cuffed with zip ties.

'I remember screaming in pain, which I was a bit embarrassed about afterward, and hearing the yells from fellow activists as they protested, loudly, about my brutal treatment. At least, as I limped off to the cop van, supported by a rather tall police officer, I managed to get out the line "Oh, my chiropractor is going to be so mad with you!"

'Actually, I think it was a commandeered bus. I was sitting with a few other arrested activists and just not being in pain was a huge relief. Although I was still hurting from my injuries, having the source of infliction removed did give me relative peace. Five, maybe six, activists went to hospital that day with various injuries.'

PB: 'You went to hospital?'

JR: 'Yeah, when we got to this rather ornate cop shop called the *Palais de Justice,* I went straight to the front of the queue, was quickly processed and sent to hospital. We had a few standard tests, but I don't recall any serious injuries. I think I had cracked or bruised ribs. At least going to hospital meant I was one of the first to be freed. I guess we must have gone for a beer somewhere. There's nothing like that sense of freedom, but I was exhausted from the ordeal.

'It's a beautiful building, the Palais de Justice. I'd recommend a visit. But if I were you, I'd content myself with viewing it from the outside.'

PB: 'When I was arrested in Brussels, we were taken to some big barn-like building, large cells with a dozen of us in each. A footie match broke out in ours with a shoe as the ball.'

JR: 'Which action was that?'

PB: 'It was an international business conference. We shut all the entrances and only allowed in the companies that were taking climate action.'

JR: 'Were there many entrances?'

PB: 'Loads, twenty, thirty, I can't remember. Each door had a team with a hydraulic pump within expanding pipes that went across the door and someone chained to it. When the police came to our door, they simply smashed the pipe out with a sledge, then removed the person locked to it. A couple of us sat in front to try to block their way but the cops just dragged us away. I rolled into a ball with one arm in front, one behind so they couldn't cuff me.

'My hand was only inches from an officer's boot and the thought flashed through my head, *I can easily wrap my arm around his foot. This would be a very bad thing to do.* At which point, the copper knelt on my head. I was unpleasantly surprised at just how painful this was and quickly offered them my hands for cuffing. They then picked me up and took me to a bollard, throwing me at it, legs either side. Thankfully, I landed before meeting the post.'

JR: 'They didn't beat you up then?'

PB: 'No, they leave that for long-haired hippies like you.'

JR: 'Then onto the police station?'

PB: 'Not immediately. They sat us in the road, hot summer's day, for about two hours, in a stress position–'

JR: 'Stress position?'

PB: 'Legs either side of the person in front, hands cuffed with zip-ties behind your back, in the crutch of the person behind. At first they made us stay upright, but after two hours, we were lounging all over the place.'

JR: 'Then what?'

PB: 'On a bus, processed in a big hall, then cells for an hour or two before being shoved back on the bus and dropped off in the middle of the city.'

JR: 'That was it, no return to court or anything?'

PB: 'Nope. Foreign ones, they usually just want you out of the country.'

JR: 'Have you ever experienced police brutality in the UK?'

PB: 'Not me personally. But then I'm a white, middle-aged male so my experiences will be quite different to people of colour or even women. If we recognise our privilege and have the freedom to speak out, surely it becomes our moral duty to do so.'

JR: 'You'll be going back to Belgium then, for the next one?'

PB: 'Ahh, maybe not.'

PNR Bake Off

I wander into the cavernous interior of Ant's rented barn, an agricultural construction of breeze block and tin around a skeleton of steel girders. It's filled with the detritus and debris of a practical hoarder – someone who can't throw away anything that one day might be useful. For years, the shell of a 1950's railway goods carriage had sat at 45 degrees, propped up on a sturdy wooden beam with a "safety" strap looping around one of the girders. In one corner of the barn is the plastic hull of a motorboat, with a stainless steel tank and wicker chairs poking out from the interior. Along the back wall, the dismantled roundwood frame of a compost toilet lies across a corrugated iron Anderson shelter. Just inside the door, a bucket collects rain from a hole in the asbestos cement roof. It is cool inside and smells of moulding cardboard. An area had been cleared in the middle of the barn, just in front of the carriage. I had volunteered to spend two weeks working on Ant's latest project.

'Here's the plan,' he says, steering me towards a flip chart leaning against a pile of broken down pool tables. 'We're going to cut out all the non-structural and rusty bits of the railway carriage.' He points to his sketched designs, 'Then rebuild it into a luxury kitchen.'

'Why? I always thought the carriage was going to be your apocalypse escape pod.'

'Change of plan. Have you seen *The Great British Bake Off*?'

'We don't have a TV.'

'You should watch it. This project will be combining two of my favourite things, cooking and activism. Greenpeace are going to do a show on the site that's being prepared for fracking near Blackpool and we're making the props. Luke's coming down in a bit to run through it, but for now we've got angle grinders, boxes of discs, goggles and gloves so let's make a start.'

We set to cutting and it soon becomes clear that it will take days to get through all the metal work. Ant orders a gas torch and bottles, it will arrive tomorrow.

Luke pulls in to the yard. He is an actions logician for the environmental organisation, early thirties with a dry sense of humour. A logician is a bit like a magician in that they make seemingly impossible things happen. Luke's turned up jeans reveal colourful socks to counterpoint his serious expression. After greetings he opens his laptop and runs through the plan.

'So it's going to be a celebrity bake off,' he says, 'on the field at Preston New Road.'

I look up at Ant and Luke, both expressions are serious. 'Who's the celebrity?' I ask.

'Emma Thompson and her sister Sophie.'

Emma is a Greenpeace supporter and a year before had helped park a giant animatronic polar bear outside Shell's London HQ.

Luke continues, 'The important thing is that it's got to look like the TV show, so we have to get the aesthetic right.'

Ant jumps in. 'The colour palette will be pale blue with a copper backdrop made from an old water cylinder.'

Luke smiles. 'I did a recce last week. Basically, I wandered around the garden centre which backs onto the field. And I'm there taking photos on my phone and the owner of the centre comes up and says "Wot yer doing?" Now I can either lie, unconvincingly, or tell him the truth, so I said that I'm with an activist group and we're planning a protest. He said, "Oh in that case, carry on." Here are the pictures.' He brings them up on his laptop. 'A green field, no crops, just grass. But here you can see the gate we're hoping to bring the carriage in through. It's chained up and heavy but I reckon, four or five of us can lift it off the hinges.'

'Can you zoom in on the grass?' I ask. It's a nitrogen fed monoculture, probably dairy. 'And this is where Cuadrilla are planning to drill?'

'Yes.'

Already I'm wondering what an angry farmer might do if a bunch of activists turned up to have a picnic on his field.

'Have they bought the site?'

'Leasing from the landowner, but they've got an injunction out, any protestors entering the field risk contempt of court.'

'So Emma Thompson is going to break an injunction?'

Luke looks up. 'We're hoping Cuadrilla will want to avoid the publicity.'

There is a lot of rusty metal to cut away so when the gas torch turns up, we huddle around Ant's phone to study YouTube videos of how to safely use it. Then Ant has a go while I stand back.

Whoosh. Get the flame right, approach the steel, sparks, lots of sparks, then bang, pop, pop, bang. I'm now hiding behind a girder. He perseveres for a while then turns the gas off. 'Sod that. I'll watch the videos tonight and try again tomorrow.'

The next day the gas bottles are loaded back into the van to be returned.

We complete the cutting with angle grinders but we're already halfway through the second week and running out of time.

I'm looking at the skeleton of a carriage and wondering how it will become a mobile kitchen. 'What's next?' I ask.

'Next we load it onto that.' Ant points to a large, triple axle trailer parked in the yard. 'Pam' (neighbouring farmer) 'is coming up this afternoon with a tele-handler. For now, we'll rub down the wooden panelling which will go back in the end sections.'

The deep throb of a large motorbike announces the arrival of Dennis. He is in his sixties, has grey hair tied back in a pony-tail and a West Country accent. Ant has got him making interior units from the broken pool tables and he's come up to check on progress.

'You've got a bit of work to do there, boy.'

'Don't worry, Dennis, everything's in hand,' Ant says.

'What about the ovens?'

'On order.'

'Ovens?' I ask. 'Plural?'

'Yeah, have to be two for the competition. They're coming from Slovakia.'

'What! Slovakia, why?'

'Have to be wood burners, with big, glass fronted ovens, chrome finish. There's only one model that fits the bill and they're out of stock in this country, so they're sending them over.'

'Wait, wait.' I raise an accusatory finger. 'You're having two ovens sent all the way from Slovakia? Hardly low carbon is it?'

'They were being sent anyway. Instead of going to the showroom, they're coming here.'

'And presumably, another two will go to his shop.'

'Yeah I know, I'm a massive hypocrite. But these will be re-used after, it's not like they're only doing this one job, and everything else in this build is recycled. We have to be sure the stoves are safe. We don't want to blow up Emma Thompson, do we?'

I look away with a tut. 'When do they get here?'

'Should be here next Thursday.'

'Cutting it a bit fine,' says Dennis.

'I ordered them last week.' Ant turns away, walking back to his jobs list on a white board. 'Should be halfway across France by now.'

After a weekend break, I'm back in the barn on Monday morning. We're joined by Rob, the heavily bearded chippy, who is constructing the floor. Barry, the Cockney painter, is rubbing down the metal frame and wiry Mark is varnishing Dennis's units. Ant has rented a holiday let nearby and we'll be staying there for the next week.

Ant holds up a tin of enamel paint. 'What do you think?'

'It's very, umm, purple.'

'Maroon,' he corrects me. 'Closest match I could get to the livery of Western British Railway of the late fifties.'

'Yeah, I can see why that's important,' I say nodding.

'Hey, don't take the piss you.'

'Have the ovens crossed the channel yet?'

He gives me a hard stare. 'I've been talking to the agent, really nice guy, done me a discount deal when I explained it was for a film. But now he tells me there's a hold up with customs because they're coming from outside the EU.'

'How long to get here?' I ask, following him to the back of his van.

'A week.'

'But we have to get it to Blackpool this weekend.'

Ant collects a cardboard box of flue parts. 'I've asked him to expedite it, what more can I do?'

I groan. 'Are you not worried?'

He turns to face me. 'After Russia?' He raises an eyebrow before walking away.

I know what he means. Two years previously, he had spent two months in a Russian prison facing the possibility of fifteen years for piracy after a Greenpeace action. Ant's perspective of worry had since changed somewhat.

Work progresses well with the talented people we're working with. As the days count down, the perfectionist joiners have to make time-conscious compromises and the addition of a toilet cubicle, built from the Anderson shelter, hanging off the back of the carriage, seems extravagant.

'We have to have something for Emma to take a piss in,' Ant says.

But the result is invaluable as it will also house the batteries, inverter and charge controller for the solar array that is to power the lights for filming.

The wooden side panels and curved tin roof are painted a deep green. Stove flue pipes are fitted for the ovens that still haven't arrived.

It's time to wheel the carriage and trailer out of the workshop. We're all looking at the top of the door.

'It's not going to fit.'

'It's too tall, Ant.'

'We'll have to take the stove pipes off,' he replies.

As Ant reverses his van to connect up the trailer, we unclip the pipes. As he pulls forward to the big double doors, it's clear it's not going to go through, it's still too high.

Ant jumps out of the van. 'Right, get the big angle grinder.'

'You're not going to cut the top off the carriage are you?'

'Don't be daft, I'm going to cut a section out of the barn.'

With wilful abandon and complete disregard for the terms of his lease, he saws through the beam forming the door header and cuts out a rectangle of the tin wall.

'Now it'll fit,' he says as we survey the wreckage overhead.
'Won't your landlord mind?' I ask
'I'll put it back afterwards, no one will notice.'

It's the end of the week, the lighting and an awning have been fitted but the solid fuel stoves have not yet arrived.
We stand around the carriage as Ant holds court. 'The action date has been pushed back three days so we have until Tuesday.'
'Is that because of the ovens?' I ask.
'No, something to do with Emma's schedule.'
'Convenient.'
Ant's smile leaves me wondering what to believe.
He continues, 'I'm told the ovens are on their way, so if anyone can stay on for the weekend?'
Rob and Mark have to head home but Barry and I can stay. Mark will rejoin us for the action.
Ant brings out a card folder. 'So you guys will be the kitchen crew. You will be going on to the field— if you're happy with that?' We nod. 'Then you'll need to read this.' He hands us each a legal briefing on two sheets of A4 detailing the possible crimes we will be committing and their maximum sentences.

Saturday and the ovens have entered Europe. We finish off painting details and plumbing in washbasins.

Sunday and a channel crossing is reported.

Monday and Ant gets a phone call from the lorry driver around midday, he cannot find us. Ant gives him directions and the ovens finally turn up half an hour later. The neighbour's tele-handler is called in again to lift them into position and we do a trial burn in the stoves, getting them as hot as we dare to burn off any residues. Then close it all down, strapping up the big side doors and preparing for the trip up north.

Tuesday and Ant is driving the Land Rover towing the trailer with the carriage while I follow in his van. We arrive in Blackpool late afternoon and as we check in to the Travelodge, I spot Emma Thompson, wearing a big white puffa coat, being ushered through reception by John Sauven. We are given an update from Luke. It will be an early start the next morning, the gate will be removed before dawn and the carriage brought in soon after. We will be responsible for getting the kitchen set up, stove fires lit and solar array in position.

Wednesday, early half light and the chill of a clear April morning as we pull into the field. People are already here, setting up marquees. We unhitch the trailer and move the Land Rover away, open up the carriage and arrange staging in front.

By the time the solar panels are set up and wired in, the day is warming up and the farmer drives past in a tractor laughing and waving at us, seems to be in a good mood. The gate is replaced and padlocked. The police turn up around the same time as our celebrities. Cameras click as Emma Thompson climbs the gate, potentially breaking the injunction, and comes over to inspect the kitchen.

'That looks fantastic!' she says. Her sister Sophie is already here and soon they are both helping to put up floral bunting and dressing the stage.

The farmer comes back in his tractor. He gets out by the gate to speak to the police and a Greenpeace manager. He stomps to and fro in his green John Deere overalls, raising his arms as he shouts something in our direction, his mood seems to have deteriorated.

The stoves are lit and prepped for baking as filming starts. With my work done, I ask a campaigner if anything else is needed.

'Can you find the photographer?' she says, 'and run his memory card back to the Travelodge for the press team in room 210? Thanks. Take a push bike and get some rest, nothing's going to be happening here for a while.'

After picking up the card, I cycle back to the hotel and in room 210 give it to the two people on laptops. I find a spot to have a little snooze, allowing myself an hour and then search out a coffee to bring me back to life.

When I cycle back, there have been developments. The police have entered the field as well as a small group of private security who hang around looking at the ground mostly. There is also a member of the public who has turned up wearing a fancy dress police uniform and pig mask. The whole place stinks of manure and there is a fine coating of slurry over the tea urns.

I see Ant. 'What happened?' I ask him.

'Farmer came around with a muck spreader. Circled twice, covered everything.'

'Not the cakes?' I spin around to the kitchen.

'No, they're fine. Sophie was holding her nose though.' Half a smile crept across his face.

We watch the masked protestor being gently turned away by Greenpeace management.

'Who's he?'

'No idea, came along, mouthing off.'

'Not a good look.'

The man takes his mask off as he walks back down the road. A call had gone out to locals to come along and take part, but then, you never know who's going to turn up.

'What about these guys?' I point to the security.

'I think they're Cuadrilla but they just stand around as if they don't know what to do.'

Luke is nearby. 'Have you seen their eyes – proper dilated,' he says.

In the tents, the final scenes are being filmed and we are encouraged over to join the cheering for the winner of the bake off – Emma with her wind turbine inspired cake, as judged by a couple of Lancashire's Frack Free Nannas. Slices of each are handed out and I have to say, both being delicious of course, but Sophie's solar power cake swung it for me.

After the celebrities leave, the atmosphere on site changes. Afternoon clouds drift over and everything feels darker.

There is a commotion by the gate. The farmer is back and he's accompanied by a farm-hand in a four wheel drive machine towing a massive trailer heading for the gate. It's clear they intend to block it to prevent the exit of the railway carriage. Ant is over there and stands in front of the machine. As soon as it stops, activists sit down in a line to block its progress. I run over and join them. The security men grab Ant and try to drag him from the machine but he holds on to a bar. With four of them on him they manage to pull him away but Ant is not a small person and holds his ground a few feet from us. They try to wrestle him but it's as if he's glued to the spot. One tries to get him in a headlock but Ant is too tall.

The farmer jumps into his tractor and starts spraying cow manure again. John runs over and grabs a tarp to try to prevent the shit fouling the equipment. As everyone watches this, Ant slips the grip of security and rushes over to help John. The farmer must still have some sense as spraying people with slurry might be called assault in some courts and he turns it off.

With only us sitting like puddings in front of the machine, the operator simply puts it in reverse and drives around us. Our blocking action now redundant, we get up and walk back to the carriage where Ant is watching the trailer being positioned across the gateway.

The railway carriage is his baby, a variety of dreams in his head for years. He was billing Greenpeace for labour and parts on the understanding that he kept the carriage afterwards. He had put so much into it, gone overdrawn to make it happen, and we had spent weeks making it beautiful. Now it was trapped in an angry farmer's field. There was always going to be this risk.

'We can stay with it overnight if necessary,' Mark says.

'I'll stay with it,' Ant says. 'No need for all of us. I'll talk to John, he'll have to approve it.' John is standing beside a tent with the campaigner and Ant goes to speak to him.

I wander over to a young policeman.

'You saw what happened there, with those security goons, wouldn't you call that assault?' I ask him.

'They're allowed to use reasonable force if acting on behalf of the landowner.'

'I see.' I notice Ant returning and meet him.

His face is tight, lips pursed. 'We have to leave it here.'

'Did you tell we're prepared to stay—'

'Yes, I told him.' The discussion is closed.

The campaigner comes over. 'We need to leave. The police have said that if we don't go now, we'll be arrested.'

'I suggest we collect up everything we can carry,' Ant says.

So anything movable, the solar panels, batteries, picnic equipment and tents are passed through a gap by the gate. The police are getting restless and by the time the last bench is evicted, the Actions Director, who has been stuck on the road side of the gate all afternoon, is urging us out. I take a last look at the green and purple carriage, standing alone in the field of lush, nitrogen fertilised and slurry sprayed grass.

Footnote:
Following discussions between John Sauven, the farmer and Greenpeace solicitors, presumably revolving around the definitions of possession and theft, the railway carriage was collected by an uninvolved third party and eventually returned to Ant. It now forms a stage for the innovative Sustain Theatre in South Wales.

Boxupants

A message arrives from Greenpeace, "We need a small number of people who are comfortable being in a small space for a number of days, for the climate emergency campaign. There is a very good chance that you will be arrested and the charges may be serious. Are you interested?"

I get a little tingle knowing that I have been chosen specifically for an event. The requirement to make at least two, five hour trips to London is annoying but, what the hell, I'm game for anything that fights for the climate.

A few days later, Ant calls me up. 'What's your availability over the next few weeks?'

I tell him I can make a few days and arrange to meet him at his workshop later that week.

As I walk down the track, his new workshop comes into view and I can see he has finished the timber cladding on the walls. It's a sizeable barn with a tin roof built around a round-wood frame. I also notice a large rusting container sitting by the front doors. Ant is walking towards me.

'Anthony,' I ask a little too slowly, 'why is there a big metal box parked outside?'

'That is a Groundhog.'

'Of course it is. What's a Groundhog?'

'It's a mobile storage unit, has a hitch so you tow it on site, then the wheels fold under the body so can't be stolen.'

'And why do you want it?'

'Give us your phone.'

I hand him my ageing smart phone and he chucks it on the van seat along with his own. We are into secret squirrel territory and my tummy tightens at the prospect. Phones are a security risk, apps can be covertly embedded that record conversations without you knowing, usually in an attempt to sell you something later but may also be used by security services. Slamming the van door he returns to me.

'We're going to fit it out so two people can stay inside for a week and you're going to be one of them.'

My eyes widen. 'I am?'

Ant is smiling, I know him well enough to sense he's not being serious. He has no say over who will be in the box.

We stare at the grimy interior. The floor is giving way, revealing rusty beams, and the paintwork on the steel sides is peeling.

'Why would anyone want to stay in there?' I ask.

'To block a doorway.'

'Oh, I see. No, I don't. Which doorway?'

'Can't say.'

My mind flicks back to the unusual request. 'Is it for...'

Ant smiles again.

We set to work, pulling up floor panels and cutting away rusty sections. We both realise this is going to take some time, and that is something we don't have a lot of.

The first trip to London and I'm surprised there are just a few of us, most I recognise. Paula, Trish, Immy, Chipper and a dozen others. Jeff is also here, we had been through many actions together and on meeting, do the manly hug thing.

'What's all this about then?' he asks.

'I have a sneaking idea,' I reply, 'but we should wait and see.'

We gather in a small back room sitting in a loose circle on fold out chairs and a couple of wooden benches. Lurking ominously in the corner is a flip chart with a blank page. The Action Co-ordinator (AC) is sitting on an upturned bucket as the Logician comes in after putting her phone in the steel box with the rest. Together they run through the plan, while trying not to mention the target name.

'We're going to shut down all entrances to the head office of a company we're calling, Bluebell. There are six doors in total, we're going to block them with heavy steel boxes and we would like you fine people to be inside them, two per box.'

Nervous glances are exchanged, a few smiles. I furrow my brow in fake consternation, I had seen this coming.

'What if we trap someone inside, isn't that a bit...?' a veteran activist called Trish asks.

'There's one door, a fire door, where instead of a box, we'll have people locked in arm tubes blocking. So it will still be accessible in an emergency.'

'What have Bluebell done to deserve this?' someone else asks.

'They are one of the biggest oil and gas companies, who say they are investing in a clean future but in fact are only putting 3% of their vast budget into renewables. The rest is being ploughed into finding even more fossil fuels that we cannot afford to burn, while lobbying government for subsidies and against climate legislation.'

'Okay so this is going to be central London?'

'Yes.'

'Early hours?'

'Yes.'

'Sounds like BP.'

The Logician laughs. 'It does, doesn't it?' She folds her arms. 'We want you to think very carefully about how it would be to spend a week inside a metal box. Could you honestly do it? What do you need to make it easier?'

'A week?'

'Yes, a week.'

'Cool.'

'Is it though? Spend the next hour in groups talking through concerns, worries, what you would do if you or your partner has a wobble inside.'

'A wobble?'

'Yeah, you know, perhaps like a panic attack.'

Everyone goes quiet as we think about the scene, stuck in a small metal box with another person losing it.

165

'After you've had your group discussions,' she says. 'We'll meet back here and run through anything that you might need, make a list of items that would help you inside, which we'll probably completely ignore.'

A wasp homes in on the biscuit Paula is holding but only manages to get tangled in her hair. Trish frees the little soul and is stung.

'One last thing, before you boxupants go home tonight, we want to talk to each of you individually.'

My turn comes around an hour later and I'm sitting before the Activist Co-ordinator and Actions Logician, both women.

'Hi Pete, how do you feel about doing this?'

'Yeah I'm fine with it,' I say. 'Mentally I'm strong, I guess the privacy thing is a bit of a worry.'

'In what way?' the Logician asks.

'Going to the loo mainly. I guess that's the same for everyone.'

'Yeah, of course. We will build in privacy curtains or cubicles, that sort of thing.'

'I'm working on one with Ant, I think we'll have space for a toilet area.'

'Any other concerns?'

'Not really.' I stretch my back. 'Should be... interesting.'

'Indeed,' the co-ordinator says. 'A lot of work has gone into it. Okay, thank you, Peter. Get yourself off home, and ask Jeff to pop over please.'

It was a couple of weeks before I could get back down to Ant's workshop, some 50 miles away. On my return, the scene is quite different. Steve, from a nearby unit, has taken on the project management as Ant has to deliver another project which involves raiding his neighbourhood for plastic recycling and getting his wife to steal supermarket shopping trolleys.

Steve works at two speeds and let's just say they are at opposite ends of the spectrum. I'm given the task of figuring out, procuring and installing the 12v electrical system, as well as some rudimentary plumbing. Steve is meticulously fitting insulation, plywood lining and di-bond cladding. A chippy in another unit is busy making internal furniture. There are only a few days remaining before the delivery deadline and things are not progressing with the speed we need.

'Why do these things always come down to the wire?' I grumble, staring at battening for the exterior cladding, hanging off the sides.

'Don't worry,' Steve says. 'I'll stay here as long as it takes to get it finished.'

Ant strolls down the track towards us. 'The welder's coming tonight to put these on.' He's holding two beautifully polished ships deadlights, like portholes but instead of glass, a cast iron cover with clamps on the sides. 'We need to cut holes in the sides.'

'Why?' I ask.

'That's how you're getting in and out.'

'Crawling through one of those?'

'You should be able to do that, Pete,' Steve says. 'Not so sure about you though Ant.'

Ant is considerably bigger than me. 'That's alright,' he says, 'I don't have to.'

We discuss where to put the circular deadlights, decide one on the side and one in the roof, and set to work with a variety of power tools.

One day to go and everyone is at the workshop, the welder has done fine work on the deadlights and is finishing up some strengthening brackets. The internal panels are being fitted. Ant's wife and mum are varnishing the plywood. Dennis is fixing car seats inside and drilling holes to give us the option of bolting the box to the pavement. Steve is working flat out to get the exterior finished, and Ant's brother is waiting to spray the whole thing battleship grey.

It doesn't take me long to wire in the lights, fuses, extractor fans and charge controller. Well, actually it takes me a couple of days, and I still have a solar panel to fit on the roof to keep our batteries charged for the possibility of a week with nothing but Jeff and an Ipad for entertainment. The panel neatly hinges over the deadlight in the roof.

Ant isn't sleeping and in a late night text exchange, has fallen out with the Action Co-ordinator. He's switched his phone off and is refusing to turn it back on. The box was due to be delivered on Saturday morning and as Friday slinks into summer's dusk, there is still plenty to do.

'Don't worry, I'll stay here until it's done,' Steve says again, pulling hard on a roll-up. I think he's developing a nervous twitch.

'I have to get some sleep,' Ant says. 'I'm driving to London tomorrow first thing.'

I volunteer to stay and help Steve.

Midnight comes as we're panelling over the rear doors. This proves trickier than expected. An early hours chill creeps upon us as we measure the end sections with bleary eyes and mistakes are made to the soundtrack of flat profanities.

Steve drops me off at Ant's home around 4.30am. An hour and half in bed then up again to return to the workshop. We connect the bolt-on tow hitch and hook it up to his van. The trailer wheels and running gear have all been professionally checked out and serviced, which included pumping the tyres to around 40 psi. We later find out that this was dangerously inadequate, they should have been nearer 100 psi.

Ant decides to take A roads rather than the motorway but it isn't long before we feel an uneasy swaying from the rear. The trailer is close to the maximum towing capacity for the van but as we hit 50mph, the swaying makes me grip the door handle and I glance over at Ant who is trying to slow us down.

'That's not good.'

'No, it's not,' Ant replies, pulling over onto a garage forecourt.

I let him think through various solutions, my brain still awash with slumber.

'Back to the workshop,' he says, 'drop the box off, you stay there and have a kip, I'll run over to Swansea and get a car trailer.'

I make myself almost comfortable on a festival stained mattress on the mezzanine. I think I sleep a bit, some rest for sure but an early summer morning with so much excitement afoot is not conducive.

Ant returns a couple of hours later and we load the box/trailer onto the car trailer. Now we are running very late and we dive into the van to head off towards the motorway.

Over the Severn Bridge and onto the M4, we have been travelling for around 40mins when suddenly there is a bang from the back.

We pull onto the hard shoulder and Ant dodges traffic to inspect the blown-out tyre. It is red hot. In our rush to get away, the trailer hand-brake was left on. Fortunately it's a double axle trailer and he manages to get the wheel off, using his massive cordless impact driver, burning a thumb in the process. We limp off at the next exit.

Parked up, we throw every bit of liquid we have at it. Fizzy pop boils, orange juice and water do little to cool the hub down. We consider urinating on it.

Eventually it cools enough to fit the spare but now the hub wouldn't rotate, the brakes have welded together. We will have to continue with just three wheels carrying the weight of our steel container.

The day is gently passing us by when we eventually turn into the industrial estate and Ant decides it's time to switch his phone on. He hands it to me.

'Better call AC,' he says.

I dial his number.

'Hi, it's Pete on Ant's phone, we're about half a mile away.'

AC clears his throat. 'Hmm, as we haven't heard from Ant all week, we had to take the decision to stand him down.' There is a short pause then AC continues. 'But as you're here now, we'll go back to the plan.' The call ends.

'What did he say?' Ant asks.

'Ahh, he'll see us in a minute.'

We turn into the storage site. The AC is waiting with a face like thunder.

'I think we need to have a conversation,' he says to Ant. They walk away into the middle of the yard and I go to find the Activist Co-ordinator who is chatting to the Logician.

'How's it going Pete?' the Co-ordinator asks.

'It's been a very long day, after a very long night.' I rub the back of my neck.

'Your eyes are quite red.'

'We're here now. Any chance I can be in this one?' I poke my thumb at the box we've just brought in.

She looks down at her sheet of names. 'We'll look at that, nothing's been decided yet.'

The next day, the rest of the activists arrive and we are split into pairs. Jeff will be joining me. We've known each other for years and he is easy company, even if he does snore a lot. We will be in the box I helped build after I list the technical requirements of the occupants. Hydraulic rams have to be pumped up then a rod releases two pins allowing the wheels to fold under the box. Bolts then have to be removed from under the floor so that the tow hitch can be taken away. It is also the biggest box, with 100mm of insulation against the others that only have 50mm. It has bunks and a separate toilet cubicle, all made from CNC cut plywood. In comparison to the small, basic alternatives, it's luxury and we name the toilet "The West Wing."

We are issued T-shirts and have photos taken. We practise getting in and out of the box which requires diving head first through the porthole in the side. We get told off for still wearing the T-shirts as they might get dirty. As I sit inside our could-be home for the next week, something hits me – the smell. The varnish on the plywood interior is still drying and the VOC's (volatile organic compounds) are over-powering.

'I'm not sure I can spend even a day in here,' I say to Jeff, my throat drying out.

'Yeah, me neither, what do we do?'

'Ant,' I call out through the port-hole, 'I think we have a problem.'

'What's up?'

'Stick your nose in here, what do you smell?'

Ant's head appears. 'Varnish. Is it bad?'

Jeff and I nod.

'Shit. I'm really sorry.' His head disappears. 'PAT, is there a shop 'round here we can buy a fan?'

'ANT,' I shout after him. 'GET ONIONS.'

His head reappears. 'Onions?'

'Yes, onions and shallow bowls of water.'

Half an hour later and the box has both portholes propped open with two desk fans blowing the air out. Bowls of halved onions and water cover every surface. We cross our fingers and hope.

After lunch we spend the afternoon on a patch of grass trying to figure out the smart phones – for pictures and video, bat phones – for communications, and radios for even more communications.

Each box team is issued with all the essentials for a week's survival including an Ipad, not loaded with the films we requested but with Rue Pauls Drag Race instead. There are interesting vegan food options, a first aid kit, containers of water and a Portapotti. We are also given a battery powered hammer drill, bolts and epoxy glue so we could fix our boxes to the ground if necessary.

That night we retire to a Travelodge under a cover story, I can't tell you what it is but eyebrows are raised in the restaurant when they run out of the vegan option.

I am sharing a room with Jeff and my heart sinks as he settles into a deep and very loud snore. I think about the week ahead until my over-tired head eventually succumbs to sleep.

The next morning we're back at the box and inspecting the interior. The onions have worked their magic and the smell has gone.

More activists arrive. They are going to be sitting on the boxes, locking across the fire exit (so that it could still be used in an emergency) and other logistical tasks. We are introduced to videographers, photographers and media folk.

We practice our roles and minute details of the early morning deployment are examined. Pictures of survivors of climate related disasters are pasted onto the sides of the boxes. For transit, these will be covered by plain sheets with magnetic strips to hold them on. Unfortunately, no one had told us about this part of the plan and di-bond is aluminium – not magnetic. We would have to skip the cover and hope the pictures stay on.

At last we are ready to take the boxes to their overnight holding positions. Ours is the only one on wheels and will be towed by a Land Rover, the rest are loaded onto lorries with hiabs.

I'm in the back of the Land Rover as we drive into London, every five minutes checking to see if the box is still following. On some of the A roads, the traffic speeds up and I notice Ant starting to wrestle the steering wheel, countering the weave from behind. I remember to breathe when we stop for lights.

Jeff is looking out the back at a car flashing at us. 'I think we've lost one of the pictures.' A sheet is flapping, half torn away. We don't have far to go and from now on, it's crawling speed so no further damage – or traffic hazards, are sustained.

The vehicles are parked and we make our way to our overnight accommodation. A 4am taxi is booked and sleep is more wished for than attained, although the unmistakable sound of Jeff's snoring proves at least one of us is getting some rest.

3.45am and I am woken by the alarm clock. We quickly dress and as nerves start to squeeze internally, use the loo in preparation for internment. The taxi takes us through dark, deserted streets to a leafy suburb. As quietly as we can, we load our personal bags and ourselves into the box/trailer. We are wished a last 'Good luck,' as the porthole is closed and screwed shut. Jeff and I strap ourselves into the double car seat for the journey.

It seems to take forever. We sit in the dark with just a faint chink of light getting in from outside. Every stop, 'Are we there?' Every start, 'No, not yet.' I'm listening for any sounds from the axles, I really don't trust them, and soon enough a repetitive clunk is heard. Every bump has me gripping the seatbelt, then, when nothing collapses or falls off, I try to relax by resting my feet on something large and yellow. Ant's very expensive impact driver had found its way inside. Finally, finally! We stop and Patrick's voice comes over the radio, 'Okay chaps, we're at the holding point. Keep it silent, we're just around the corner from a cop shop. Over.'

Now it's waiting. Waiting for everyone else to get into position. Waiting with sweating palms and legs that won't stay still. We don't feel the cold night around us. Over in box number four, Imy and Paula have taken travel sickness pills not knowing they were maximum strength and have both fallen asleep. We hear the Land Rover engine start and we're moving again. Seconds later Patrick calls us, 'Get ready, we're almost there.' We unclip the seatbelts and switch on the internal lights, readying ourselves for action. The Land Rover stops, reverses, the trailer wheels hit the curb and the Land Rover tyres start to slip. The vehicle pulls forward and back again, this time with more speed, we hit the curb. Again the tyres lose traction. Someone, (it might have been me) had put blocks of wood in the back of the Land Rover for just such circumstances.

I can hear the regular beeps of a telehandler in reverse, removing another box from a lorry while around the corner, a hiab (a crane fixed to the truck bed) swings a box just inches over the top of a parked car.

With the blocks in place, we mount the curb and shuffle into position. At the holding position, I had removed the floor panel and undone the bolts holding the tow hitch on. Now I had to knock the bolts out as it's being unhitched.

I can hear Ant outside, 'Have you got the bolts out?'

'Nearly... that's it, bolts out.'

The square metal section slides off and disappears.

'Right, now pump.'

I grab the lever that jacks the wheels off the ground and pump up and down as fast as I can. I can hear police sirens approaching.

'Police are at the road block,' says a voice over the radio.

'Pump faster,' says Ant.

'I am pumping faster,' I yell back. We are rapidly tilting at an angle as the hydraulic pistons push the front up. We're almost at 40 degrees and Jeff is having to stop himself from sliding down the floor. I'm starting to slow so he takes over.

'Okay, stop.' Ant says. A rod is pulled and pins release the suspension, allowing the wheels to retract. 'Now down.' I turn a small lever and we start to sink. 'No stop, back up again.' I can't believe it, something is wrong. I push the lever back and start pumping again. 'Okay, stop, that's enough. Now back down.' We sink again, this time going all the way to the pavement.

We're there, we're in place. No we're not.

'Hold on,' Patrick shouts. 'Just going to nudge you into position.'

The Land Rover suddenly rams the box and it scrapes noisily over the paving stones.

Patrick calls to Ant, 'That's it, perfect, the door's totally blocked.'

The Land Rover's engine fades away.

New sounds now, voices outside, people on the roof. Police sirens entering the square.

'Cup of tea?' asks Jeff.

'Rude not to,' I reply. We take a picture, determined to be the first image sent to the outside world, of us drinking tea at five in the morning.

After breakfast, Jeff falls snoringly asleep. I read for a while. Every now and again I hear police outside muttering options and every time one of them tries pulling the now redundant wheel release rod. It's the only thing they have to play with.

173

Greenpeace have published a plan to help wean BP off oil and gas, so when Jeff wakes, we make a short video pretending to be shopping channel hosts.

'Hi, Jeff, what do you have there?'

'It's a ten point plan, Pete.'

'A ten point plan, what does that do?' For some reason, I have an American accent.

'It's to help you get off them nasty fossil fuels, would you like one?'

'I certainly would, Jeff. But where can I get one?'

'They're absolutely free! Just pop on over to the Greenpeace website and pick up your very own.'

I try to send it over to the media number but it won't go. The steel container isn't helping the signal but we were getting a connection earlier. I check the 'bat phone' – our name for the basic Nokia used as a clean line, no signal on that either, it's possible the police are blocking our communications. The radio has been quiet for some time but that only has a short range.

Jeff decides he needs to use the portapotti. Being a boatie, he's very used to the arrangement. We also have a bucket of fine sawdust for urine, and when I installed the 12v electrics, I made sure there was an extractor fan in The West Wing.

Occasionally we hear snatches on the radio when people are communicating within our range. It sounds like the climb team are having a hard time. They are trying to attach letters to spell out, CLIMATE EMERGENCY, over third and fourth floor windows but the fixings are failing. Fortunately they have a banner as back-up.

We have lunch, a boil in the bag effort. We're a bit concerned about lighting gas in such a confined space so double check the CO alarm that's fitted next to the smoke detector. It works and the meal is a pleasant surprise. We are quite comfortable in our steel pad but now that the sun is overhead, the box next door, which only has 50mm insulation, is getting really hot inside.

A voice on the radio, 'They're breaking in!'

Jeff looks at me. 'That's not good news.'

We had hoped the police would take a more cautious approach and wait for us to get bored.

An hour or so passes and we start to hear metal banging from down the street.

I press my head to the roof hatch and call to the people sitting on our roof, 'What's happening?'

'Looks like they're cutting through the container doors. I think we're being told to come down. Yes, we're going to have to leave you now, good luck.'

'Thanks, you too. Bye.'

Another hour as police work on the boxes, one by one they are broken open. Then they come to ours. They've removed the thin plywood cover to our entry hatch and are trying to smash the deadlight in, but the welder has done a very good job, it doesn't budge.

'You hungry yet?' says Jeff.

BANG, BANG.

'Not really, bit early for tea isn't it?'

BANG, BANG.

'Yeah but once they get in, no telling when we'll get fed.'

BANG, BANG.

'True, get the burner on.'

Another boil in bag down and the police have given up trying to bash their way in. They are drilling the rivets off and you can sense their frustration on finding a complete steel container beneath the di-bond and plywood coverings.

We get a little peace and quiet until an angle grinder starts up. Sparks are flying inside and the smell of burning paint and metal fill the box. We push a mattress and pile things against the lengthening cut. Not very sensible fire prevention but at least it keeps the smoke down and we know we have another exit hatch. We stand in the middle facing each other.

'So much for the week's holiday in the Costa del Plywood,' I say.

'I know,' Jeff says. 'I was actually looking forward to some down time.'

'So what do we do now?'

'Options?'

'We can lift a floor panel and slide underneath, or go out through the roof hatch or stay here and wait for them to come in.'

Jeff studies the floor for a moment. 'Hmm, GP might not want us hiding out.'

'So the roof is a compromise?'

'I'll see if I can get through to AC.' Jeff picks up the phone, still no signal. Next he tries the radio. No response.

'Here, one bar.' I've got the bat phone held up to the port hole in the roof.

Jeff takes the phone and sticks his head against ceiling. 'Hi, yeah it's us. They are about to come through the wall, what should we do?'

'What did he say?'

'I think he said stick it out, but I can't be sure, with the noise and all.'

'So does that mean up or down?'

Jeff shrugs.

'We haven't got much time, they'll be through in a minute.'

'Ahh, underneath?'

'Okay, underneath.'

We fill our small rucksacks with items we don't want the police to keep forever, which for me includes Ant's very heavy impact driver.

Sim cards are taken from the phones, broken in half and chucked into the blue sludge of the portapotti. I lift the floor panel, throw a sleeping bag onto the pavement below and lower my legs through. They get tangled in the sleeping bag and won't go any further.

'This isn't going to work,' I announce.

'Roof then?'

'Yep, roof.'

I pull myself out of the hole and jump up onto the top bunk. Undoing the two clamps, I swing the deadlight cover back revealing the underside of the solar panel. 'Get that bit of wood there.' I point to a short length of four by two and Jeff passes it up. A screwdriver is acting as a locking pin, I pull it out and use the timber to push up the hinged panel. Wedging it in place, I crawl through the hole to emerge into the early evening air. A cheer from somewhere down the end of the street, as I look around I can see friends and familiar faces behind a police cordon. John Sauven, the executive director is there and the AC. I give a slightly foolish wave and then hear a metallic clang as the police finally break in so quickly turn to help Jeff out. He hands me our bags, before squeezing himself through the hole.

We take a tour of the box roof. Below us are very annoyed officers of the law. One strides past, dressed in overalls indicating a specialist of some kind.

'This is not what we expect from Greenpeace,' he shouts at me.

I shrug my shoulders. 'Lack of communication.'

'He's not happy.' Jeff is standing beside me.

'What now?'

'Always assume there are cameras pointing.' He holds up an A3 sized notice, "BP, STOP WRECKING OUR CLIMATE." We stand there until I get bored and sit down.

I stretch my legs out. 'We're definitely going to get arrested, so may as well stay here for a while.'

'Yeah but look.' Jeff points towards the other boxes. 'We've shut down their head office for the day.'

'Pity it wasn't longer. I was starting to enjoy our little stay.'

'It was a bit claustrophobic.'

'And you snore.'

'Do I?' Jeff takes a step back and opens his hands in fake surprise.

We are called to either side of the box and two young officers arrest us from the ground, reciting the familiar caution.

Half an hour passes. I take a look over the back of the box. There is a gap of about half a meter enclosing a confined space against the door we are blocking. I ease myself over the side. A police officer is watching me. 'If you do anything like that, you'll be resisting arrest,' he warns.

'Just looking,' I say and climb back onto the roof.

Another man in overalls addresses us, 'We're going to have to rig up safety lines to get you down. Will you consider coming down a ladder?'

I lean into Jeff. 'Are we achieving anything staying up here?'

'Not much, but look it's 7.15, I think Channel Four news finishes at 7.30 so just in case they have a film crew down here, let's ask for 15 minutes.'

'I'm okay with that.'

Jeff calls down, 'Give us 15 minutes and we'll come down on a ladder.'

They agree.

The early summer evening is starting to feel chilly as we climb into the police van. As usual the two officers try to engage us in conversation.

'Have you come far today?'

They always ask this, it must be in a training manual somewhere. It sounds like idle chat but we know they are fishing for information. They look like they're in their early twenties and I wonder if they have children, loved ones to worry about with an uncertain future. Do they even understand the slow burning fuse of peril they – we all, are facing?

I stare out of the window. 'Don't mean to sound rude, but I'm just going to enjoy the view.'

We arrive at the station and wait in a holding cell, all four of us, for about 40 minutes. Our arresting officers are well past the end of their shift and are getting frustrated by the delay. One of them goes to find out the reason – I suspect we were forgotten about – and we are finally taken to be booked in. I'm frisked and pockets emptied. The Desk Sergeant is a woman in civilian clothes. She opens my bag and takes out the big yellow tool, it thumps on the desk. She looks at me with one eyebrow raised.

'It's an impact driver,' I say, as if that explains everything. She humphs and makes a note.

After the paperwork, I'm taken to a cell and I settle down for a snooze.

A metallic slap from the door as the viewer is opened and a key in the lock. It's the middle of the night.

'Your solicitor is here. Come with me,' the officer says.

Bleary eyed, I walk down a brightly lit corridor and into an interview room. My solicitor cheerily introduces himself and we quickly run through the "no comment" procedure.

'You're the most relaxed person I've seen,' he says.

'I'm still half asleep,' I reply.

The official interview is the shortest I've ever had. After the preliminary name and date of birth, the officer reads out about eight questions to which I answer, "No comment" every time. Setting up the recording machine and unwrapping of disks took longer than the interview itself!

We were released under investigation at around 5am, and Neil, one of our trusty support team is waiting to collect us.

'Would you like breakfast in a café or straight back to the office?' he asks.

'Is it too early for a beer?' Jeff asks.

The Woman in the Red Dress

A shiver of anticipation fizzes through every single body in the room. The words, "interrupt the Chancellor, Philip Hammond live on TV" had just been uttered and the mission laid clear, to deliver an alternative speech, one which takes the climate into account.

It's the evening of a prestigious annual dinner for accumulated holders of wealth and power in the UK, at the Lord Mayor's official residence, Mansion House* and Greenpeacers are going to try to gatecrash it. The thirty women and half dozen men know they may be forcibly ejected by security if they do manage to gain entry but no one is expecting the subsequent media storm.

Activists are split into teams and shown a diagram of the room layout. One team will try to take the microphone from the Chancellor and read out the alternative speech, while the rest are to give neatly presented paper versions to guests. Janet's team is to go to the right hand side of the room and she is also given the task of filming the protest on a mobile phone.

The men dress in tuxedos and the women in matching red dresses that have been made specifically for the action by a talented dressmaker. Excited voices as they dress and prepare. How often do you get to glam up before an action? Before they set off they practise the order in which they are to enter the room. The door openers and blockers first, followed by the speech makers and banner holders. Next it's the leaflet deliverers, they are expecting to enter the building in single file so everyone has to take note of who they are standing next to.

They take the underground to Bank Station and walk a short distance to a church. Timing will be crucial to the success of the action so they need somewhere to hang out, waiting for the right moment. A caretaker lets them into the church as they pretend to be a choir and are led in vocal warm up routines. Their voices fill the large, circular space, bouncing off cool limestone and timber benches.

Janet whispers to Helen, 'I feel flipping awkward about this, it's cheeky but so necessary.'

'I know what you mean,' Helen says.

'If we get in though, it'll be worth it. Getting right in there, it's such a ballsy action.' Janet looks down at her shoes, she knows it's a really important thing they're going to do but there's a child-like reluctance to burst in on "important" people. She looks back up at Helen. 'We've got to do this.'

They continue with the La's and Lo's until it starts to feel excessive. The caretaker pops his head in from time to time to make sure they're alright. Next they each read a poem. Janet reads Benjamin Zephaniah's Nature Trail; which obviously strikes a cord with many.

As others read, Janet plays with the catch on the little handbag she's been given, inside is a "CLIMATE EMERGENCY" sash. *This is taking too long,* she thinks.

They've been waiting over an hour now and the tension is mounting, surely it must be soon.

The Action Co-ordinator gathers everyone together. 'It's almost time, we've got a holding position outside the venue, so we'll go there now. Everyone stay in your teams.'

They all follow her out of a secluded back entrance to the church, which leads to a quiet area near Mansion House. It's a warm night but Janet is feeling a chill through the thin dress material. Anxious glances are exchanged, general fidgeting and hushed conversations. Immy is trying to distract herself by listening to a bird calling over the drone of traffic.

Minutes pass. Janet thinks how odd they must all look, hanging around, dressed the same. Immy checks her phone, 20.58.

'Sashes on,' the AC says, 'and fast walk.'

Thank goodness we were told to wear flat shoes, Janet thought.

They scramble to put the climate emergency message over their shoulders and follow the AC, making sure the top table team are in front to give them the best chance to get in.

Suddenly the AC stops. 'Turn around, we can't get in this way.' The weight of disappointment hits Janet like a stone in the stomach. 'Shit, is that it, all for nothing?'

'Plan B,' the AC says.

Phew, there's a back up.

They follow her around the building, in through a door. This was different to the route they had scorched into memory so the layout would be different and they would have to think on their feet once inside.

There are stairs, they take them two at a time, the deep plush carpet exuding wealth beneath their shoes. They reach a landing. Ahead of them are numerous doors all facing the same way, so they spread out and pour through, into the grand, glittering dining hall. It's much larger than Janet expected and packed with extremely well-dressed people. All very intimidating. Just inside the doors are smartly dressed staff who are surprised to find these people rushing past and for a moment are caught in indecision. Immy's team turn left and head for the microphone Philip Hammond is attempting to use.

Janet goes for a door on the right and is confronted by a young man in a suit.

'You can't come in.'

Janet jams her foot against the door. 'Oh come on, please? We've got a really important message, and just have to deliver it.'

For a split second, he hesitates. Janet slips through the gap and under his arm. She walks quickly off to the right hand side to orientate herself in the room. This is where her group are to gather but when she turns, she realises the remainder of her team haven't made it in. She is on her own amidst stunned guests sitting in their splendour, white table-clothes, silver service and candelabras.

On the other side of the room, the top table team is blocked and so Hannah is loudly reading the speech, surrounded by security. One of the male Greenpeacers, a Canadian, spots the Governor of the Bank of England, Mark Carney and hands him a copy of the speech.

Janet takes her phone and, standing in front of a row of tables, starts filming. After about a minute, she looks around and realises no one is paying her much attention. She glances over to the Chancellor who is waiting for the commotion to be expelled. Janet also has the speech, wax sealed, in her hand.

It looks like I'm the only one here who can still give this to Philip, I have to give it a go.

She turns and, as calmly as she can, walks around behind the tables. Her head is swimming and heart pounding at the enormity of what she's doing when suddenly a chair is pushed out into her path, an arm shoots out and a large furious man pins her against the wall.

Shit, there goes my chance. The disappointment distracts from what's actually happening. He takes her by the neck and arm, marching her back towards the entrance. Janet is thinking that this man is taking it too far, he must be really angry so she tries to focus on de-escalation, even though his grip is starting to hurt. She notices some TV cameras off to her left and wonders if someone is filming.

'This is a peaceful protest,' she says, but he doesn't let go. They reach the doors and a woman in black, presumably security, offers to take over but the man declares he intends to see her off the premises.

Out through the door, he holds Janet's head forward as they go down the stairs, putting her off balance. She is desperately trying not to fall.

'It's okay,' she says. 'You can let go now.'

He doesn't respond and his grip doesn't loosen.

She tries again, with a little humour 'Look, you can let go now. What do you think I'm going to do, wrestle you?'

'I'm not letting go of you,' he splutters, almost struggling to get the words out, 'until you're outside!'

At the bottom of the stairs, the main entrance is being guarded by a woman, who holds the door open as they approach. The man pushes Janet by the neck, out into the street saying:

'This is what happens when people like you interrupt our dinner.'

Janet swings around staring into his bulging eyes. The words for a stinging comeback are missing-in-action, so she holds her phone camera up, pretending to film him. Her trembling fingers incapable of switching it on.

He is gone. Janet is standing on the street. She looks around, unsure what to do, but then sees a familiar face from Greenpeace.

The woman comes over and says, 'I've seen you, make your way back to base.'

Janet takes off the climate emergency sash, goes down into a tube station and stares at the map for a few minutes, her mind is too busy trying to process what has happened and she cannot redirect it to figuring the route back.

Eventually she works it out and is on the underground train to Islington. Her head is reliving the events while her body is dealing with a loaded nervous system. She notices her hand is shaking as she puts it over her mouth and squeezes overflowing eyes tight shut.

How will this look from Greenpeace's point of view? I shouldn't have gone off like that. Shit, am I going to be in trouble for going rogue?

When she gets back to the office, others are also returning and the mood is celebratory. A photo is being organised in reception but Janet doesn't feel like joining in and goes looking for a cup of tea. She meets up with her team who confirm they couldn't get in the dining hall and are a bit miffed to have been shut out but still buzzing with the excitement of being involved.

'What happened to you then, Janet?' Helen asks.

'I got forcibly evicted. Thrown out. I did some filming, probably poor quality. I've still got the phone, I had better give it to media.'

Back in the warehouse, a large screen is set up and everyone gathers to watch the footage on the news. Cheers at having successfully got the message across and to get immediate media attention is pretty unusual. Everyone is swapping stories of their experiences.

Janet remembers the phone and heads off towards the office when someone stops her;

'Are you alright?'

'Yeah, I'm fine,' Janet replies. 'Why?'

'Because that guy who pushed you. ITV news filmed it and now there's a twitter storm, it's gone crazy. Do you know who he was?'

'No idea.'

'Mark Fields, a Tory minister. That's why it's gone crazy. Would you like to see?' He leads her to the press office. There's a small group huddled round a monitor showing a news report and footage capturing the assault.

Janet stares at it, it seems unreal, the cameras she'd noticed had in fact been rolling and the assault looks pretty forceful. It's obvious just how angry he was.

It's late now and beds are found for activists who cannot make it home. Janet is sharing a room with Immy who is scrolling her smart phone.

'My gosh,' she says. 'This is really kicking off, it's going to be massive.'

'Oh no. I'd better phone Pete, let him know.' Janet tries to call me but I've gone to bed so she leaves a message.

The next morning, after not much sleep, Janet opens her eyes and lies still staring at the ceiling. She knows today could be pretty crazy and hesitates before switching on her phone. Ping, ping, ping, everyone is trying to get through to her, news agencies, reporters, friends and family.

I get up late and when I switch my phone on, ping, ping, ping. Multiple missed calls from Janet.

I phone her. 'What's wrong, what's happened?'

'Have you seen the news?' Janet asks.

'No, why?'

'At the do last night, some minister knob grabbed me and it was caught on camera.'

'Are you okay?'

'Yeah, got a bruise on my arm. I was a bit shaken—'

'Janet, you should have called me.'

'I tried! You'd switched your phone off. Anyway, it's turned into a right media scrum so you might get some hassle. Greenpeace are advising us to take down any online content, not to comment on social media, that sort of thing. The gutter press is already harvesting pictures of us off Facebook, one described you as an author.'

'Ha, where did they get that idea from?'

'And apparently we live on a farm. Better go, John Sauven is heading this way.'

'Good luck.'

The Executive Director checks on how Janet is feeling and that she is being looked after. He then asks if she is going to take the matter further and report it to the police. Janet is unsure, on the one hand she acknowledges she took the decision to go into a situation which might get rough and accepts the consequences, but on the other, should she stand up against physical abuse of women? John advises her to think it through carefully.

Newspapers have traced Janet's phone number and are trying to get through so she puts her phone on silent and goes to see the media team. They warn her to give her mum a heads-up and sure enough the *Daily Mail* have already doorstepped her for an interview. Luckily Janet's mum is pretty savvy and backs her daughter up, telling them how Janet has always been for the environment.

Graham is in the press office, Janet has known him for years so she asks for advice on whether to press charges.

'It's entirely up to you,' he says. 'I can't tell you what to do.'

Janet walks to the window overlooking the rear garden. 'I don't want to drag this on any longer than it has to, with the right wing media labelling me a snowflake.' She turns back to Graham, 'And I don't want the message of why we were all there in the first place to get lost in this mess. I think I'll let people make up their own minds.'

He approves, 'Trial by public opinion.'

Janet agrees to an interview with *The Guardian* as the journalist is known to be sympathetic. She is offered a Greenpeace T-shirt to wear but doesn't want to look corporate, being told what to say, she would be more comfortable in her own. Unfortunately the only clean one she has left has *Count Duckula*, a children's cartoon character, on the front. She does the interview and is photographed in the garden.

The journalist asks, 'What do you think should happen to Mr Fields?'

'I would like him to go on an anger management course and I hope he doesn't do it again, there was some serious anger there. But for me the concern is the environment, always has been.'

Here in Wales, the media have found out where we live and are hunting for interviews. Luckily, we live along a private lane and our neighbour, who is working in his garden, intercepts the journalists and gives me a warning. Although I go to speak to them, I have no quotes they can use. If I feel like I'm under siege, Janet is getting it worse. TV crews are camped on the Greenpeace office steps and she is under pressure to give them something. After agreeing to answer three questions, with her stomach churning at the thought of facing actual TV cameras wearing a Count Duckula T-shirt and little make-up, she bumps into Veronica.

'Any advice on what to tell them? I'm crapping it.'

'They're saying you could have been armed, so you can say that you were only armed with peer reviewed science.'

'That's good, yeah.' Janet smiles, remembering. 'I was at the Climate Camp action at Heathrow where we held up signs saying that.'

After the interview on the steps, Greenpeace smuggle a very relieved Janet out of the back gate and into a waiting Uber to take her to Euston station. She's desperate to be back home but concerned someone might recognise her. No one did.

I am worried that the press might still be hanging around. They had been knocking on doors throughout our village hoping to dredge up gossip on us, so I'm ready to collect her from our local station but by the time Janet arrives, about 8pm, they have all gone home. The next day, the news has moved on to Boris Johnson's big argument with his girlfriend.

Footnote:
Mark Fields was immediately suspended from his position in the Foreign Ministry and not re-appointed when Boris Johnson took over as Prime Minister. He later stood down as the Conservative candidate for the Cities of London and Westminster, in the following election.

Despite Philip Hammond claiming the government was leading the world in its commitment to become carbon neutral, the Climate Change Committee reported that the government is still missing all its targets.

Extinction Rebellion

"Just saying it could even make it happen," goes the line in the Kate Bush song, *Cloudbusting* and it's reverberating through me as I wake up back home after spending six days in London with Extinction Rebellion.

For over 30 years we've been saying we must cut greenhouse gas emissions to prevent global overheating, but just saying it doesn't make it happen. For the last six days we've been protesting for governments to take action on the climate crisis and ecological collapse.

"We'll introduce a law to go carbon neutral in 30 years time," they said, but just saying it won't make it happen.

The chants that repeatedly rang around my ears for the past six days have been, 'What do we want? Climate justice. When do we want it? Now,' and 'Whose streets? Our streets. Whose planet? Our planet. Whose children? Our children.' And whenever someone is arrested, 'we love you, we love you.' Could just saying it even make it happen?

For one of these chants, it certainly does and it's a powerful part of Extinction Rebellion. Right from the opening ceremony, I realised that something was different here. The atmosphere is charged with energy, respect and love. Focussing on the collapse of nature and the fight for survival our children will be facing, brings raw emotions to the surface. I've seen grown men standing in a crowd, fighting back tears for no apparent reason, hell I'm even doing it now just thinking about it. Occasionally it even seeps through to the police standing guard over us for hours on end. With my arm in a steel tube, chained to another soul as the police line edged closer, a procession of figures all dressed in red with white face-paint, slowly, gracefully, arrive, a hushed quiet falls. It's a bit spooky, it's a bit disturbing and for a reason I can't explain, very moving.

They position themselves between us and the police, silently facing the officers, their gestures and faces pleading, I watch a female officer chewing her lip and eventually, swiftly wipe away a tear. Then, without a word, the Red Brigade turn and leave. Several hold out their hands to us as they walk past and looking into their faces I can see where tears had streaked the white paint and I understand.

These moments are rippling all around and through the rebellion. As we sat there, Sian and me, locked together, people came up to offer food, chocolate, donuts. Complete strangers were thanking us, hugging us, kissing us. Complete strangers looking out for each other, protecting each other. And in front of us, two silver-haired grandmothers in their seventies lay in a tent on the road, chained into a similar arm tube, and that's where they spent the night, alongside us.

Trying to sleep on a London road with the constant threat of arrest is hard. Trying to sleep with a helicopter hovering feet above your head at three in the morning is hard. Disrupting people just trying to get to work is hard. Standing your ground with a tool of the state demanding you move is hard. But a glimpse of a world where generosity is valued more than greed, where courage brings love and a common, desperate purpose brings unity, makes it, just about, worthwhile.

Yes there's dancing and laughter too, spirits have to be maintained in the face of fatigue and fear and grief.

This is the last throw of the dice, the last chance to evolve the human race beyond the cul-de-sac of our own stupidity. Do not be deceived by the naysayers and down-players, even the ultra conservative International Monetary Fund has published a paper in which the authors say that, "the risk of catastrophic and irreversible disaster is rising, implying potentially infinite costs of unmitigated climate change, including, in the extreme, human extinction."

Powerful messages perhaps but it's all just words, stories we tell each other as we shelter in cocoons of nine to five jobs and supermarket shopping. Not until it all falls apart will those words take on their full, terrible meaning.

And as for that last chant, 'we love you', you might dismiss it as being hippy, or perhaps a bit too soppy, but whether it's sitting around a family breakfast table or on a wet street in London, yes, just saying it can even make it happen.

Insulate Britain

Emerging from Extinction Rebellion, Insulate Britain hit the headlines by shutting down major motorways around London in the Autumn of 2021. Saving energy and lowering people's heating bills should be an obvious step to making a considerable reduction in carbon emissions except it costs money, even when it's shown that investment in insulation is a saving in the long term which benefits all.

Despite energy efficiency being campaigned for since at least 2010, government efforts to insulate Britain's leaky homes have been piecemeal at best. With time fast running out for the climate, these campaigners felt drastic action was required and so, putting aside popularity and focussing on maximum disruption, they stepped out on to the M25.

A contact who, for legal reasons, has to remain anonymous, agreed to answer a few questions for me:

PB: Can you tell me how it feels moments before you walk out to block a motorway and what is it like standing in front of angry drivers?

Anon: I know others find it nerve wracking but with experience it's no big deal, safety is always our priority. Traffic is stationary at red lights so you just walk out and stand in a line holding the banners. Walking out in front of a lorry doing 15mph is a bit livelier but I didn't feel it was dangerous as the driver could see me and had plenty of time to stop. The rest of the team quickly followed as the traffic was coming to a halt. As mentioned below, angry drivers are a distraction as you need to keep an eye out for the safety of other activists but most run out of adrenaline after five minutes of venting their anger, it is important to have the de-escalators continually engaging.

PB: You say safety is a priority, what if an ambulance is trying to get through?

Anon: When we blocked the main carriageway, the hard shoulder was left clear to allow ambulances or fire engines though. On roundabouts the outside lane is blocked by activists but they don't glue to the road and on two lane junctions, again one lane is left unglued.

PB: Many people say that you are wrong to target ordinary folk going about their business, how would you respond to that?

Anon: Our protests need to be put into perspective as there are 608 events on the M25 every year that lead to huge traffic congestion, we're only blocking until the police respond. I think the longest was about 90 minutes until all were removed from the main carriageway. We aren't selfish, we don't want to be there, we are doing it to wake up the government to the 8,500 lives lost every year due to fuel poverty, and climate change is going to break down civil society – now that will be a disruption to ordinary folk.

PB: How do you feel about the threat of a prison sentence?

Anon: Our aim was to go to prison on remand to embarrass the government, and I tried, by being arrested five times in the first two weeks. I wasn't overly bothered about it and expected two to six weeks but a political decision was made not to jail any activists only weeks before COP26. Two rebels have made it to remand, one due to his previous record and one because he glued onto the police custody desk and then tried to do it again. I was not prepared to break the injunction banning blocks on certain roads as the fine can be limitless. So a proper prison sentence for that was never a possibility.

PB: Can you describe, in your own way, a memorable Insulate Britain moment?

Anon: The first time we blocked an M25 off ramp at a set of traffic lights, the response of drivers before the police arrived (30 mins) was very hostile, pulling banners off us, swearing at us, shouting at us, we were pushed and pulled. But our response was completely peaceful and we held our space with our two de-escalators continuing to engage quietly with drivers, I was very proud to be a part of such a focussed, calm professional team.

PB: Has there been a significant event in your life that led you to this?

Anon: Not really, it came from the frustration that not enough is being done to combat climate change, I have tried everything else in the last 12 years!

The 18 days I was with Insulate Britain has affected me, I do wonder how we can simply go on with day to day living when such a catastrophic future awaits. We have made a difference by being continuously in the news (despite the bias shown by the right wing media) and now some are bravely breaking the injunction. Morally we are in the right and we are showing up the government for its lack of care for us all.

Also being in the company of such kind, dedicated, supportive people has been uplifting.

I think the government will have to step up its response as Insulate Britain is a thorn in their side, hopefully they will overreact so the world will notice.

Footnote:
At the time of writing, eleven Insulate Britain protestors have been jailed with terms up to six months. One of them, Emma Smart then went on hunger strike for 26 days. Seven others were given suspended sentences with costs awarded against them totalling £39,000. Several have vowed to keep protesting.

A Trojan Horse

In the seventies, racing cars would be plastered with adverts for the tobacco industry. Today, sponsorship deals between oil companies and cultural institutions seek to legitimise operations we now know to be contrary to the health of the world and one day, these too may also be banned. BP was sneaking its branding into the British Museum under the guise of a sponsored exhibition about ancient Troy, so what better metaphor to protest this advertising than a wooden Trojan horse? The challenge was taken up by *BP or not BP?* A group of actor-vists who literally made their name by jumping up on stage ahead of BP sponsored Shakespeare plays and performing a short act culminating in a plea to the audience to take the programme and rip "out damned (BP) logo."

"Help us bring a Trojan Horse to the British Museum's Troy exhibition, to kick out the dirty oil sponsor BP!" was the message on the crowd-funding page. There is to be no secrecy about this action.

My mate Phil called me over to his place in Oxfordshire to talk through the design of the horse. I love the idea but he is working in a tiny garage to a tight schedule and I worry that the finished piece won't have the wow factor required. It will be built around a metal frame with a sheet of 8'x4' plywood forming a kind of table-top. The horse's body is to be made from old pallet wood into a barrel shape which will neatly lower over the table to reduce height in transit and then raised into position using a system of ropes and pulleys, giving a space within for several people. With only four weeks to complete the construction, I volunteer to help despite him living three and a half hours away.

Then Boris calls a General Election and the project is postponed until the following February.

'He's got plenty of time to do it now,' I say to Janet after she asks about Phil's progress. Winter is a busy time for our business, so I'm unable to get back over to him.

Early February. The horse is stabled in London in a small unit south of the river. Ant has been brought in to drive the towing vehicle and supply a sound system, so we go over to see how Phil's doing.

The horse is still not finished, but it's looking incredible. Phil has been working non-stop for a month and is now joined by a small team carpenters, labourers and artists.

I know Jess and Danny from my Oxford days, but I hardly recognise him with his beard and woolly hat. His eyes are wide and staring so I give him a bear hug.

'This is the biggest thing we've ever done,' he says. Danny has a very expressive face and at the moment is looking slightly crazed. 'There's 1,500 people coming Saturday and I have to organise stuff for them to do.'

Jess is being super cool, arranging last minute details and briefing everyone that will be helping in the morning. They are planning three major actions for the weekend, a day of mass participation, an overnight occupation and the horse. With the date broadcast on the campaign website, inviting the public along, the museum will be expecting them and have increased security. They will have to try to sneak the horse in a day early, on Friday.

A friend of Phil's who mixes sound for films, has prepared horse noises on an Iphone 4 and I plug it into the sound system to check volume. A very loud equine snort confirms it's working well.

The last of the planks are being added and the tail, made from old hemp rope, is attached. The head, with illuminated red eyes and blowing smoke, is the last and finest bit of sculpture, to go on. It takes about seven of us to lift and slot it into place. The plan was to travel with the head off but nobody wants to go through the pain of taking it off and on again. The problem is that with it on, the body becomes significantly heavier and the pulley system still hasn't been made. It's 9pm and the horse needs to be galloping through the British Museum's courtyard in nine hours time. The only option left is to see if we can lift the body by hand. I reckon it weighs about a quarter of a tonne.

Two lengths of four by two are slid under and six people get on each piece. We lift, it goes up. Keeping it up is painful but we've proved it can be done so it comes down again.

The metal frame has wheels on each corner with the front pair steering via ropes threaded under and behind. Phil has even constructed rudimentary brakes for the rear wheels. The doors to the world are opened and the Trojan horse is led out. At around 10pm, some very tired people eventually ease the creation onto a car trailer, cover it with a very large tarpaulin and depart for the night. Phil beds down with the horse to keep it company, under a damp railway arch.

Next morning, 5am start. Drive across London, pick up the trailer and head over to the British Museum. Gathering around the corner from 6.30am.

There are few people around so we slowly unload the horse to allow Ant and the transport to clear off. Accessories, banners, Greek shields are propped up against railings outside someone's house and we try not to make too much noise. Giggles break out and I move a few yards away, leaning nonchalantly against a lamp post. I don't think the arty folk are used to undertaking potentially illegal actions and are a little too boisterous for my liking.

There is a last minute hitch – there usually is. The letter to the museum director, revealing the action, has been lost, possibly on the street last night. This means, (A) someone may have picked it up and alerted the staff, (B) we have to find someone to print off another. Jess is on the phone and manages to persuade someone to climb out of bed and come down to meet us with a replacement letter. We'll just have to cross our fingers on the other thing.

Enough people have now arrived for us to lift the body and Phil takes charge. Once up, brackets are fitted to securely hold it in place and we are ready to set off.

With eight people pulling on ropes from the front and others pushing from the rear, we wheel the horse around the streets of central London, at one point overtaking a resting double-decker bus. Phil is steering on the "reins" at the back but needs someone else to operate the brakes.

'Who's got a driving licence?' he asks.

We come to a side gate to the museum that the horse has been built to fit through.

Three plans have been drawn up. The first is to gain entry through this gate (I cannot say how), second, if entry is not available, wheel it to the front gate and ask politely to be allowed in. The third is, if not allowed in, park it in front of the gate and work from there.

Circumstances are smiling on us, we get in through the side entrance. Phil is so overwhelmed by fatigue and the moment that he forgets to turn left, he is almost steering the horse into the museum wall. Reverse a few paces then try again.

It is with relief and elation that we round the corner within the courtyard of the British Museum, knowing we have made it, there is nothing anyone can do to stop us.

Jess is over the moon. 'We're in! We've made it.' I can't see her but I can tell from the break in her voice that she is grinning madly. It's been a monumental effort, on a tiny budget, and no one can quite believe that they've done it. Including security by the main gate who are staring dumbfounded for a moment, their faces blank in shock, as a huge wooden horse appears behind them. They run over but it's too late. *BP or not BP?* had been quite open about bringing a Trojan horse to protest the oil firms sponsorship, but there is no doubt about their surprise at seeing the twelve foot high wooden construction being wheeled in under their noses.

The horse is parked in front of the grand façade, a wheel removed to ensure it stays put and negotiations with security commence.

Sometimes it's better to ask for forgiveness than permission.

I need to make an exit as I have an appointment at the Australian High Commission later that morning but the gate has been locked behind us. I see Paul, who I recognise from previous actions, and together we go to the front gate where three security guards are standing.

'Can you let us out?' Paul asks.

The guard gives us a quick look over. 'If you want to get back in, make sure you're wearing your pass.' He must think we're museum staff. As he opens the gate, I hear the guards behind us talking about the horse.

'But how did they get in?' one of them is asking.

I walk away towards Aldwych, to the accompaniment of the sound system booming out whinnying and robotic horse noises.

Phil and another volunteer stay inside the horse Friday night to welcome the crowds on Saturday in the largest protest the museum has ever seen. I return the next day and have to queue up for bag inspection to get into the front courtyard. Once inside, I check on the horse. The sun is shining and the Trojan soldiers of *BP or not BP?* are standing guard. The sound system battery has gone flat so I jump inside and wire in the solar panel, which helps bring it back to life. Phil's eyes are rubbed red and it's clear he hasn't slept much but after the weeks of hard work and long hours, the final rush of getting the horse in and the triumph of completion is fuelling his tired body.

'We're going to need another battery,' he informs me.

'I'm not sure how we're going to get it in, they're searching bags, but I'll talk to Ant.'

As I leave the Museum and walk back through the streets, one part of a plan is building in my head. I phone Ant and the second part falls into place. Sadly I cannot tell you how, but a 12v leisure battery is smuggled into the Trojan Horse.

Activities carry on throughout the day. *BP or not BP?* has organised talks inside the exhibition halls from international campaigners linking climate change, fossil fuel extraction, colonialism, human rights abuses and workers' rights. Performers stage impromptu shows and the song/chant of "BP must fall" reverberates through the building as the Great Court is packed with protestors.

The careful balance and respect between the activists and the British Museum bears fruit at the end of the day as staff prepare to close the doors. 40 activists refuse to leave and occupy the Great Hall overnight, stretching the protest into a third day.

All night they work making plaster casts of body parts to create a sculpture, which they name, Monument, for display to the public as they enter on Sunday.

The horse is taken away by activists at the end of the weekend, still whinnying its disapproval of the museums choice of sponsor.

The Oil Rig

"There comes a time when one must take a position that is neither safe, nor politic, nor popular, but he must take it because conscience tells him it is right."
– Martin Luther King Jr.

Wednesday 29th May 2019.
Janet receives a message from the Greenpeace Activist Co-ordinator.

'It's a boat team request,' she explains to me. 'They're asking if I can get to Inverness, by Saturday.'

'Wow, that's short notice,' I say.

'Shall I go?'

'It's what you've trained for, of course you should.' Janet had been on the boat team for three years and was now confident handling an RHIB (inflatable power boat).

'But that leaves you all the work here and I don't know how long I'll be gone.'

'I can look after things here, but you should book next week off work.'

'Okay, if I can take annual leave, I'll go. If not, I won't.'

Janet phones her boss, it's very short notice but she gets the time off. We huddle around the laptop, trying to figure out the quickest way to get to Inverness – without flying or driving obviously. There's an overnight sleeper train but it's really expensive and doesn't run every day. So she books a train straight from work on Friday that gets her into Inverness Saturday afternoon, after an overnight stop in Glasgow.

I'm curious as to what's happening near Inverness that requires such a quick response from the boat team, so hit Google and the Maritime Traffic website. It takes some searching but then I come upon an article on an oil and gas news site. BP had acquired rights to exploit a new field in the North Sea and has contracted a US company, Transocean, for the drilling. A Transocean owned platform called the *Paul B Lloyd Jr* had been moved to the Cromarty Firth, just north of Inverness, for refurbishment and is now ready to leave, the news site proudly announced. I am starting to get an idea of what is going on.

By now, Janet has reached the camping barn Greenpeace is using as a base on the Black Isle and knows what is being planned. Other members of the boat team are arriving as well as climbers, they are going to try to stop the platform from leaving for the oil field.

It has been calculated that if we burn all the fossil fuels in known reserves, the carbon emissions will take us sailing past the 1.5 degrees of the Paris Agreement and into the horror of runaway climate change. A catastrophic scenario that would almost certainly end civilisation and perhaps even the human species. Here is a company whose whole business model is based on continually finding and extracting more and more oil and gas. The Vorlich field, to which the platform is due to go, is a new project, adding 30 million barrels to the reserves we cannot afford to burn. Stopping it is the only sensible thing to do. However, we do not live in a sensible world, we live in a world dominated by the quest to make money.

Pete is on a cycling holiday around Scotland with his girlfriend when he gets the call. Luckily they are already on the East Coast and make a detour.

Every day, James, the acting AC, gives a briefing. It's looking like the platform's departure will be any day but they can't be sure. They have to time it just right, there's no point stopping a rig that isn't about to leave.

Every day, they wait and still no sign of the platform weighing anchor.

As the week slips by, Janet confides to Paula, 'I've only taken one week off, have to be back at work on Tuesday. If it doesn't happen soon, it's a wasted trip and I so want to be part of this.'

James has been watching from the cliff tops with binoculars and a VHF radio tuned into shipping frequencies, waiting for any indication that they are readying the platform for departure. Two large vessels have anchored nearby, these will be used for towing the platform and another smaller supply ship is buzzing back and forth. It won't be long now. This afternoon he is joined by Daniel.

'Take a look at that.' James hands Dan the binoculars. 'Those ships have come around and I reckon they're preparing lines to tow.'

'I think you're right, they have to raise the anchors first though.'

'Yeah yeah, it's got eight, so will take a while.'

'Do we have enough people to do this?' Dan asks.

'Just about, it's really tight. We do have more on the way though.'

At this moment a clear transmission comes over the VHF, 'Prepare to raise anchor number eight.'

'That's it,' James says. 'Let's go.'

They jump into the van and race back to the base. They estimate they have a window of about 40 minutes to get climbers onboard the rig.

When they reach base, he finds the climbers have been practising and are halfway up a wall in a tangle.

'You've got twenty minutes, get yourselves down and ready to go,' he barks.

Janet finds Paula in the shower. 'Get out, get out, we're going now!'

An inflatable boat is already loaded in the van and soon they are racing to the harbour.

'Act natural,' James says as they lower the boat into the water. Janet tries to walk calmly as she carries bags of supplies while her heart is beating out a dance track and her brain is shouting, *hurry, hurry, hurry*. She looks at the others and can see it's the same for them. Pete and two other climbers, jump into the boat while James starts the engine. Soon they are skimming over the glassy still waters of the Firth. It's late afternoon, but being mid summer in Northern Scotland, it will remain light until after ten. Janet waits onshore with the van.

James noses the RHIB up to a leg of the 27,000 tonne oil rig, alongside a metal ladder. The climbers step from the boat's rubber sides to rusty rungs and start ascending. It's a good twenty metres to a gantry that forms a narrow walkway halfway up the leg. This is where they need to be before the workers on board notice what's happening and try to stop them.

They make it to the gantry and Pete helps haul up their kit before returning to the boat. The other two, both women, stay on the platform and tie off any access points, hanging a large banner over the side; "CLIMATE EMERGENCY." The women can now take a breath. They look at each other with big grins.

'I can't believe it. We've just stopped a bloody great oil rig.'

'Aye, this is proper direct action, we're taking on the big boys.'

James powers back to the shore to swap places with Janet. He pulls the radio from his pocket and breaks into the Transocean channel.

'Paul B Lloyd Jr, Paul B Lloyd Jr, this is Greenpeace. We have just put climbers on to your vessel as part of a peaceful protest. Please stop all operations immediately. Greenpeace will not, I repeat, will not, allow you to take this rig to the Vorlich field to drill a new hole for oil. Greenpeace standing by.'

Janet and Paula take the RHIB back to the rig and position themselves below the walkway. Their job is to be on hand if the climbers suddenly need evacuation or help. Paula has long dark hair which was still wet when she donned her helmet and as the sun sinks below the horizon, is starting to feel cold despite nine layers. To keep spirits and temperatures up, they sing songs and dance around the little boat. It's an all night vigil with sleep as elusive as an oil CEO's conscience. The two women overhead are struggling to get any privacy, being watched constantly by rig workers on an adjacent platform, but exhausted from a tense, adrenaline and elation fuelled afternoon, they eventually bed down for the night.

Next morning, Paula gets a call from James.

'Police are on their way out to you in a row boat.'

'Shit.' Paula turns to Janet. 'Police are coming, is there anything we need to get rid of?'

'The map?' They have an Ordinance Survey of the coast marked with all the secret rendezvous points and places where supplies have been hidden.

'We should tear it into little pieces and stuff it in a flask.'

As they are doing this, Paula is watching the harbour. A tiny rowing boat emerges but it doesn't seem to be coming towards them. Through her binoculars she can see two old men in it with fishing rods. She picks up the phone.

'James, they don't look much like police to me.'

'Ha, ha, had you going there.'

Paula puts her hand over her eyes. 'Yes, you did.'

'Come on back and get some rest. Well done for the night shift.'

Police have now arrived and parked a van by the slipway. When Janet and Paula tie up in the harbour, they approach.

'What are you two doing?'

'We're just the safety boat,' Janet says.

'Oh... okay,' says the officer.

The women briskly walk away.

The day passes in a stalemate. The police watching from the cliffs and the Coastguard from a patrol boat. The women on the rig have deployed a fold-out platform below the gantry in case the walkway is accessed by workers. By evening they have been on the rig for almost 30 hours and don't have supplies to stay much longer.

Pete had intended to continue his cycling holiday and his partner has been waiting patiently but he is the only member of the climb team available. A second, Tom is on his way and everyone is waiting for him. When Pete tells his girlfriend that he will be going to relieve the occupation duo, she cycles off alone.

Tom arrives and is told that he has 20 minutes to get ready. He hasn't eaten all day so while others prepare equipment, he grabs some food and then they are off to the RHIB. Slipping through the water in the twilight, they avoid the patrol boat and reaching the platform leg, quickly swap over activists. Pete and Tom have provisions for days and settle in for a long haul.

Day three and an Interdict, the Scottish version of an injunction is served on Greenpeace. Rig workers try to lower the notice in a bucket down to the occupiers on the gantry but they refuse to take it. An injunction only comes into effect if the transgressors are aware of it. It is essentially a judge telling someone they cannot do something. Once told, if it's ignored, it shows contempt for the court.

Day four and Daniel is going shopping for the shore team. There is only one small store in town and he is trying to find anything that's vegan. Having cleared the shelves of fruit, pasta, dairy-free cream cheese and Bourbon biscuits, he presents his load at the till. It comes to over £100 and his card is maxed out.

'I'll just go for another card,' he tells the shopkeeper. 'Be back in a min.'

The door gives an old fashioned tinkle as he leaves and is confronted by two burly men in cheap suits.

'You are under arrest. Get in the car.' They grab an arm and steer Dan towards a dark Volvo.

'Wait, wait. Who are you? What have I done?'

'I'm DS McKenzie and you are under suspicion of being involved in the illegal occupation of an oil rig. I'll caution you when we get in the car.'

'I have to pay for the shopping,' Dan complains as he's shoved into the car.

Day five and the police have got their act together. Specialist removal teams are in a patrol boat circling the platform, figuring out the best way to get to the activists. Every day the rig is delayed is costing BP somewhere in the region of £140,000. Pete and Tom are leaning on the gantry handrail, watching the circling boat.

'They'll be doing all sorts of risk assessments, is there anything we can do to hold up the process?' Tom asks.

'What if we wait 'til they sod off, then rig lines down to the fold-out platform, make it look like we're preparing to move position?'

'I suppose they'd have to come back and re-do their assessments.' Tom points at the boat as it powers away. 'Look they're going, let's do it.'

Janet has returned to work and that afternoon comes home while I'm on the laptop.

'How's it going?' she asks, dumping her bag by the kitchen table.

'They're still there as far as I can tell but nothing on GP twitter for ages. I've been trying to find a Cromarty webcam but they're all pointing in the wrong direction.'

'Wouldn't it be awesome if they could bring one of the ships in?' She's referring to Greenpeace's fleet of three vessels.

'They could be anywhere in the World. I'll see if I can find them.'

I go back to the Maritime Traffic website and search for *Rainbow Warrior III*. It's in the Med. Next I try *Esperanza*.

'That's odd,'. I say.

Janet peers over my shoulder. 'What is?'

'It's moored in Portland Harbour, down in Dorset. Been there a while, not going anywhere.'

It is in fact, about to depart for a leg of the Pole to Pole Tour, exploring man's impact on the marine environment but it's waiting for one last crewmember, James, who is currently in Scotland.

'That just leaves... I type in the name *Arctic Sunrise*.

'Yes! It's heading up the East coast at 14 knots, that's full speed.'

Janet does a little dance. 'If only Tom and Pete can hang on in there.'

Tom has climbed down and attached himself to an anchor chain about 10 metres above the sea, forcing the police removal team to do a third trip around, re-assessing their procedures.

Onshore, a photographer and videographer are watching, cameras ready when they are approached by uniformed police.

'Would you mind coming with us please?' a tall officer wearing thick rimmed glasses asks.

'Why?' the video operator asks.

The photographer flatly refuses. 'We're independent journalists, we're allowed to be here.'

'No you're not. You're with Greenpeace,' the officer replies. 'We need to take you in for questioning.'

'No way, we're not going.'

'Right, you're under arrest...'

On hearing about this, James is worried, he phones Tom and Pete on the rig.

'Be really careful up there. They've cleared the area of photographers so it might be they're going to try something risky.'

The *Paul B Lloyd Jr* is a semi-submersible platform meaning it can adjust its height in the water. As Tom is standing on a metal bar, ten metres below the gantry, he feels a trembling through the steelwork. He looks down, the water seems to be slowly coming closer. He switches his phone over to camera and records a short piece.

'That's the police RHIB just behind me.' He jabs his thumb over his shoulder to a black boat bobbing around a few metres away. 'They are currently sinking the rig around us. You can see the water level is coming up, even though I'm attached to the metalwork.'

Turns out, they have careful control of the platform and it stops submerging with the water lapping around Tom's feet, allowing the police boat to come in close and pick him off the rig. Pete is also arrested and the occupation, after 70 hours, is over.

The *Arctic Sunrise* calls into Sunderland to pick up a German climb team and an injunction is slapped on her too. She must not interfere with BP or Transocean's operations.

At home Janet and myself, along with Greenpeace supporters across the country, who have been following the action, go to bed disappointed that it's over but happy with the attention it's raised and knowing that, just for a little while, a tiny portion of carbon intensive suicide has been delayed.

Day six, 4am. A damp, grey sky is starting to lighten. Early morning air mingles with salt and reeking seaweed. They can just about see well enough for safety and the activists hunker down into the small RHIB as the engine fires. As instructed, so not to raise suspicion, Darryn at the helm, pootles at half speed out onto the sound. It will take about ten minutes to make the transit. They are halfway when they receive a call from the AC:

'Something's happening, you need to get there fast.'

Darryn pushes the throttle full open and they start to bounce over the water. They arrive a few minutes later and disgorge their passengers.

The sun hasn't properly risen behind rain-filled clouds, when Leanne makes the radio message;

'*Paul B Lloyd Jr, Paul B Lloyd Jr,* this is Greenpeace boat *Piglet*, we have put two climbers onto your left leg, you are no longer safe to proceed, please acknowledge, over.'

'Greenpeace boat, *Piglet*, this is *Paul B Lloyd Jr*, acknowledged, we will cease operations.'

Leanne looks over to Darryn as he turns the RHIB away from the massive rig. 'I can't believe I've just done that.'

The London office takes an angry phone call from Transocean. Scottish Police are also trying to get through. An interdict has clearly been broken. The *Arctic Sunrise* is once again sailing north at full speed.

The pair on the rig manage to hold out for most of the day but the police now have techniques and paperwork in place and by late afternoon, they too are removed. Soon after, the *Paul B Lloyd Jr* is towed out of the Firth, beyond Greenpeace's reach, or is it?

Day seven and all across Britain, local groups have organised protests outside BP garages with "CLIMATE EMERGENCY" banners. Janet and I join one in Abergavenny and spend two hours enduring car fumes and curious customers. From now on, all we can do is follow the action from a laptop, watching ship movements on Maritime Traffic and twitter updates from Greenpeace.

The rig has two large vessels slowly towing it to towards Vorlich oil field and two supply ships in convoy, while the *Arctic Sunrise* is on a course to intercept.

Onshore, fourteen people, including three journalists, have been arrested.

Day eight. The *Arctic Sunrise* blocks the route of the convoy, which turns around and heads back to shore. No one knows what they are planning.

Day nine and the convoy has done a U-turn, plotting a course back to the oil field. As they plough through the North Sea, supply ships unsuccessfully try to block the *Arctic Sunrise* as she overtakes, taking up a position between the convoy and Vorlich. Once again the convoy turns around and goes back towards Cromarty.

Day ten. The convoy is trying yet again to get to the oil field. Greenpeace launch two RHIBs in an attempt to get climbers onto the rig but the sea is too choppy to get close so they unfurl banners for a photo instead. People sometimes ask, "What's the point of a banner?" Humans are visual creatures, a picture is a simple and direct form of communication. A founder of Greenpeace, Robert Hunter, would refer to a powerful image, such as the iconic photo of activists in a tiny inflatable boat putting themselves between a whaling ship and a whale, as a "mind bomb."

Once again the Greenpeace ship parks itself in the middle of Vorlich. After 500 nautical miles, going backwards and forwards, the convoy does a third U-turn and heads back to Scotland.

Day eleven. The *Paul B Lloyd Jr,* its two towing vessels and supply ships are again attempting to get to the oil field. Sarah North, Greenpeace's International Climate Campaigner, volunteers to get into the water ahead of the rig. In a press release, she says:

"For eleven long days, we have used every possible peaceful means to stop BP drilling for more oil that we can't afford to burn. Each day we've held BP off is a day we've prevented them further fuelling the climate emergency."

As she floats in the freezing North Sea, she holds a flag warning of the climate emergency. It's a photo opportunity, there's nothing more they can do.

Day twelve, resources have run out and the pursuit is called off. The *Paul B Lloyd Jr* finally lands on the oil field. Greenpeace have managed to prevent twelve days of drilling at a cost to BP/Transocean estimated at over £1million. The cost to life on Earth of continued oil exploration is far greater.

Footnote:
On February 24th 2020, John Sauven, Executive Director of Greenpeace UK, went to court for breaking the interdict. Transocean lawyers asked for unlimited fines and to consider a custodial sentence for Contempt of Court. In the end, Greenpeace were fined £80,000 plus costs and John avoided jail. BP claim they had nothing to do with the case.

Greenpeace applied for, and were granted, a Judicial Review into the issuing of drilling permits for the Vorlich field, which happened without proper public consultation. Their argument is that without that consultation, the only way to question the morality of the permits was to physically intervene, even if it meant breaking an injunction.

The government consequently admitted acting unlawfully in granting BP's permit to drill for new oil in the North Sea.

Afterword

Bathtub Climate Science

Imagine Earth's atmosphere is a bathtub. The plug is in and one tap is turned on, the tub fills with water until it reaches the overflow hole. Roughly the same amount of water flows out as goes in. The water is Carbon Dioxide, nature is the tap and the overflow. Everything is in balance. Then humans come along and discover a second tap and turn it on full. Now the overflow pipe cannot cope, the water reaches the top of the bath and eventually runs over, soaking the floor. This is where we are now. At some point, the floor is going to give way and the pipes will burst, making the situation much worse. We have to turn off the second tap.

Extract of Janet Barker's closing statement at trial December 2019 for blocking a road with Extinction Rebellion.

"I don't have kids. Me and my husband have concerns about bringing a child into the world on its current trajectory, I'm also not that maternal. I was however struck a while ago by the child of a friend of mine who with her brow furrowed in concern said; 'Did you know that whales are dying with plastic in their tummies?' I said yes. She then continued, 'Did you know Orang-utans are dying because we are cutting down their forests?' I have to say that these two sentences coming from a child really got to me. She is seven years old and instead of her spouting interesting facts about animals like the fastest, largest etc here she was genuinely worried about the future of these animals. When I was her age, I was worried about which dress to wear. What have we done to this world that children are being

saddled with this kind of worry? We are failing those that we care about the most. We are not being worthy custodians or responsible adults. It's time to be responsible now and demand that those in positions of greater responsibility look after that which we all hold dear – our home and all its inhabitants."

Everyone wants the best for their children and yet they sit idle while the future scenarios become increasingly grim. The latest science warns of the possibility of four degrees of warming by the end of the century. Currently (as of writing in 2021), we are approaching 1.2 degrees and already we are seeing Arctic Circle permafrost melting, releasing vast amounts of greenhouse gases, wildfires in Siberia, America, the Amazon and Australia, releasing vast amounts of greenhouse gases. Both the Amazon forest and the oceans now seem to be releasing more Carbon Dioxide than absorbing, and ice in the Arctic is being replaced by heat absorbing dark sea. Air one degree warmer can hold 7% more moisture, increasing heat trapping clouds. These are all positive feedbacks meaning we have set in motion a sequence of events we have little control over. But, in theory, we can still limit the damage if we act fast with drastic cuts to our emissions and ensuring we leave all fossils fuels in the ground. Let's be clear about why we have to do this. We are living through a mass extinction event, one of only six to have ever happened on this planet. A rapid change to a world four degrees warmer is not compatible with life as we know it. It would be a tempestuous place of climatic extremes – unimaginable storms, heat waves, fire and flood. It currently appears likely that we will be the last generation to enjoy whatever abundance that we cherish, be that food, shelter, technology, energy, liberty or peace. If you are in the Global North, chances are these things will come to an abrupt end. If you are in the Global South, chances are you're already struggling with them.

And yet, the collective wisdom of humanity still concentrates on making money, pointing to us being the first species on Earth to be the architect of its own demise. Unless... unless we get off our arses and... well, you know what to do.

Acknowledgements

I would like to thank Anthony and Zaharah Perrett, Janet Barker, Jeff Rice, Danny Chivers, Kev Drake, Phil Ball and Sterl for their contributions. I would also like to thank Joss Garman, Ben Stewart, Victoria Henry, Sandra Lamborn, Darryn Payne, Leanne Kitchin, Daphne Christelis, John Sauven and Len for pitching in, together with Greenpeace and all the other activists who have helped make this possible.

My special thanks goes to Nicola Ratnett for initial proof-reading and continuous support.

Half of the author's royalties from sales of this book are being donated to groups that fight for environmental protection, including but not limited to: Greenpeace, World Land Trust and Survival International.